The Illustrated World of
OCEANS

The Illustrated World of
OCEANS

SUSAN WELLS

Woodland Presbyterian School

Simon & Schuster Books for Young Readers   Published by Simon & Schuster
New York · London · Toronto · Sydney · Tokyo · Singapore

5224

SIMON & SCHUSTER BOOKS FOR YOUNG READERS
Simon & Schuster Building
Rockefeller Center
1230 Avenue of the Americas
New York, New York 10020

Designed by Paul Richards (Designers and Partners). Illustrated by: Mike Saunders, Janos Marffy
(Jillian Burgess Illustration), John Rignall (Linden Artists), Martin Camm, Jim Channell, Tim Hayward,
Robert Morton, Colin Newman, David Thelwell (Bernard Thornton Artists),
Tony Bryan, John Downes, Steve Weston.
Created and produced by Ilex Publishers Limited. Printed in Spain.

10   9   8   7   6   5   4   3   2   1

Library of Congress Cataloging-in-Publication Data

Wells, Susan.
The illustrated world of the oceans / by Susan Wells.
p. cm.
Includes index.
Summary: An atlas of the earth's oceans, with illustrations and information about their history,
inhabitants, exploration, and uses.

1. Oceanography - Juvenile literature [1. Oceanography]   I. Title GC21.5.W45 1991
551.46-dc20   90-27361
                                                                                                    CIP
ISBN: 0-671-74128-4

CONTENTS

WORLD OCEANS

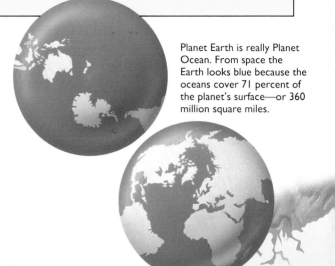

Planet Earth is really Planet Ocean. From space the Earth looks blue because the oceans cover 71 percent of the planet's surface—or 360 million square miles.

THE EARTH has more ocean than any other planet in our solar system. The oceans are largely responsible for our climate, they are where life began, and they provide us with food and numerous other essential products.

The total volume of the oceans is about 330 million cubic miles but this is not evenly spread over the planet. Most is in the southern hemisphere. There are five major oceans. The Pacific is the largest, covering 32 percent of the globe, with an area of 63.9 million square miles, more than all the land put together. It is also the deepest ocean, with an average depth of 13,800 feet, but plunging over 7 miles. in the Mindanao Trench. The Atlantic is only half as big, with an area of 31.7 million square miles. It is also shallower, with a maximum depth of 31,357 feet in the

Baltic Sea

ASIA

Persian Gulf

Red Sea

Arabian Sea

Bay of Bengal

NINETY EAST RIDGE

INDIAN OCEAN

Rain forests of the sea
Coral reefs grow in the warm, coastal waters of the tropics. They can be thought of as the rain forests of the sea because of the enormous variety of plants and animals found on them (see pages 44-45).

Puerto Rico Trench. The Indian Ocean lies in the southern hemisphere and covers 28.4 million square miles. The small Arctic Ocean is almost entirely surrounded by land, and is usually covered by ice, 10 to 12 feet thick. The Antarctic, or Southern, Ocean is larger and surrounds the continent of Antarctica. Two-thirds of it freezes in winter. Seas are smaller, shallower areas of ocean, partly surrounded by land, and include the Mediterranean, Baltic, Bering, and Caribbean.

Sperm whales
Sperm whales live in all oceans. They are the most numerous of the great whales but have been massively hunted for their oil (see pages 34-35). The head of the sperm whale is about one-third of the animal's length. Sperm whales have the largest brains of all mammals.

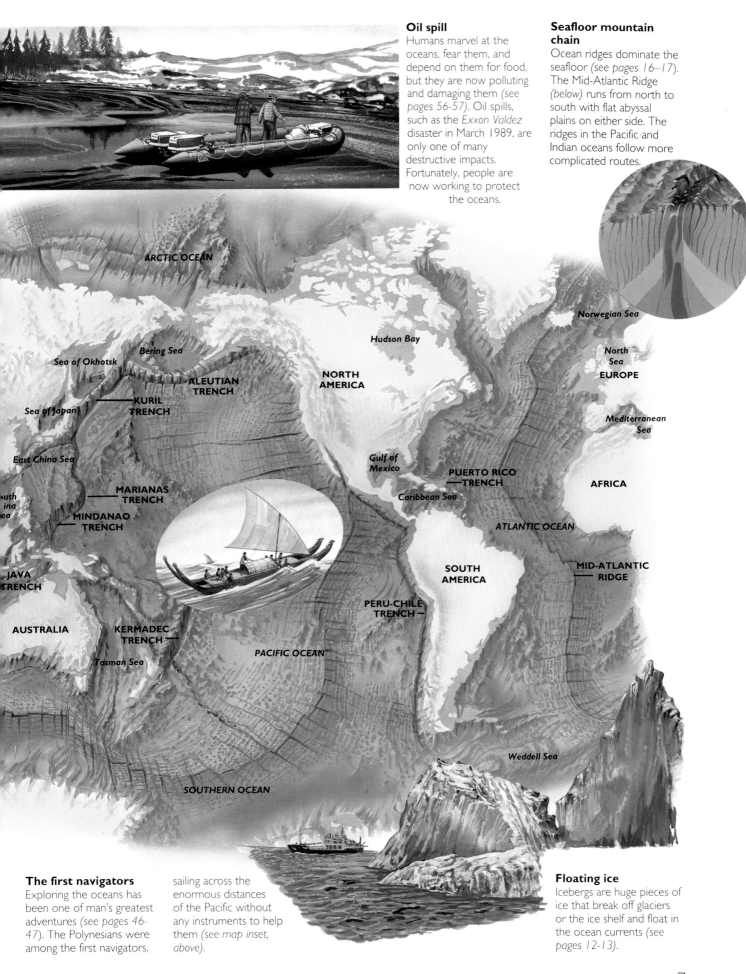

Oil spill

Humans marvel at the oceans, fear them, and depend on them for food, but they are now polluting and damaging them (see pages 56-57). Oil spills, such as the *Exxon Valdez* disaster in March 1989, are only one of many destructive impacts. Fortunately, people are now working to protect the oceans.

Seafloor mountain chain

Ocean ridges dominate the seafloor (see pages 16–17). The Mid-Atlantic Ridge (below) runs from north to south with flat abyssal plains on either side. The ridges in the Pacific and Indian oceans follow more complicated routes.

ARCTIC OCEAN

Hudson Bay

Norwegian Sea

Sea of Okhotsk

Bering Sea

North Sea

Sea of Japan

NORTH AMERICA

EUROPE

ALEUTIAN TRENCH

KURIL TRENCH

Mediterranean Sea

East China Sea

Gulf of Mexico

PUERTO RICO TRENCH

AFRICA

South China Sea

MARIANAS TRENCH

Caribbean Sea

MINDANAO TRENCH

ATLANTIC OCEAN

JAVA TRENCH

SOUTH AMERICA

MID-ATLANTIC RIDGE

PERU-CHILE TRENCH

AUSTRALIA

KERMADEC TRENCH

PACIFIC OCEAN

Tasman Sea

Weddell Sea

SOUTHERN OCEAN

The first navigators

Exploring the oceans has been one of man's greatest adventures (see pages 46-47). The Polynesians were among the first navigators, sailing across the enormous distances of the Pacific without any instruments to help them (see map inset, above).

Floating ice

Icebergs are huge pieces of ice that break off glaciers or the ice shelf and float in the ocean currents (see pages 12-13).

THE CIRCULATING WATERS

THE atmosphere and the oceans form a single system that creates weather, climate, currents, and waves. Ocean waters store heat from the sun during the day and in summer, and release it at night and in winter. This causes daily variations of land and sea breezes as well as seasonal monsoon cycles.

Currents transport heat around the oceans, together with oxygen, nutrients, plants, animals, turtles, young and migrating animals. The surface currents in the top 150 feet are produced by winds. The Earth's rotation deflects the water movement so that it flows at an angle to the wind direction. In the northern hemisphere, it flows to the right of the wind, creating clockwise currents, and in the south to the left, creating counterclockwise currents.

The North and South Equatorial currents flow from east to west across the oceans. In the Atlantic, the northern current flows into the Gulf of Mexico and then north and

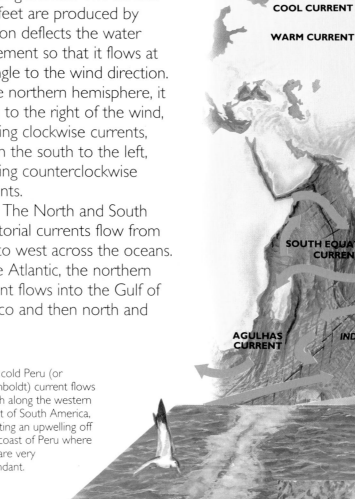

COOL CURRENT

WARM CURRENT

KUROSHIO

SOUTH EQUATORIAL CURRENT

AGULHAS CURRENT

INDIAN OCEAN

ANTARCTIC DRIFT

Upwellings
Upwellings form where currents part (divergence), or where winds blow surface waters away from the coast. In both cases, cold, nutrient-rich water is able to rise. This occurs mostly on the west coasts of continents, or in the Southern Ocean. Upwellings provide food for many plants and animals, so they are often important fishing grounds.

The cold Peru (or Humboldt) current flows north along the western coast of South America, creating an upwelling off the coast of Peru where fish are very abundant.

The visit of "El Niño"
Periodically, a mass of warm water flows south along the west coast of South America, swamping the upwelling. This often happens just after Christmas, so it is called "El Niño," or "The Child." It brings with it torrential rain, and the food chain is drastically altered. In the 1982–83 El Niño, corals were bleached white *(below, left)* and tens of thousands of animals in the Galapagos died. There were also droughts as far afield as Australia and northeast Brazil.

east as the Gulf Stream. It flows at up to 140 miles a day, with numerous complex eddies and gyres (giant circular ocean surface currents). The calm waters at the center are called the Sargasso Sea. Many animals, such as turtles, travel across the Atlantic in the Gulf Stream. The South Equatorial current flows south when it meets the coast of America. Similar circular currents are found in the Indian and Pacific oceans. There are also ocean currents that flow deep beneath the surface. Driven partly by cold,

ARCTIC OCEAN

LABRADOR CURRENT

YA WO

NORTH ATLANTIC DRIFT

GULF STREAM

Sargasso Sea

Gulf of Mexico

NORTH EQUATORIAL CURRENT

NORTH EQUATORIAL CURRENT

GUINEA CURRENT

TORIAL COUNTERCURRENT

SOUTH EQUATORIAL CURRENT

Currents carry all sorts of objects around the world. Shipwrecked sailors would send messages in bottles. Animals, like these goose barnacles clinging to the bottle, often hitch rides and become established in new areas.

BRAZIL CURRENT

PACIFIC OCEAN

PERU CURRENT

BENGUELA CURRENT

ATLANTIC OCEAN

ANTARCTIC DRIFT

Weddell Sea

dense, sinking water, they are usually much slower than surface currents. The two main masses of cold water are the Weddell Sea in the south and the seas around Norway and Greenland in the north. These sink and the cold water flows towards the equator along the bottom, gradually welling upward and becoming part of the surface currents.

Lines in the ocean
Convergences are where different currents come together, usually causing water to sink. Areas where currents part, allowing water to rise, are called divergences. In both areas, floating material, including logs, seaweed, garbage, and even wrecks, often gathers in long lines. These attract huge concentrations of animals and birds. In the Atlantic, baby turtles live in the floating sargassum weed and are carried out across the ocean.

OCEAN WEATHER

The weather at sea is very important, sometimes a matter of life or death. Apart from cyclones, tropical oceans have the lightest winds, particularly in the "doldrums" on the equator. North and south of the equator, the trade winds dominate. They blow from the northeast in the northern hemisphere and from the southeast in the southern hemisphere. On either side of these are the westerlies. The "roaring forties" are westerlies that roar around the Southern Ocean. At the southern tip of South America, they are funneled through the shallow gap between Cape Horn and the South Shetland Islands, making these among the roughest waters in the world.

Tropical cyclones form over warm water, as warm, moist air rises. They generally move westward across the oceans.

The water cycle

There is a continuous cycle of water between the oceans and the land. Water evaporates and forms clouds, which condense as rain. Water on land flows back to the sea mainly through rivers.

CLOUD GROWTH
CONDENSATION
EVAPORATION
RAIN
SURFACE RUNOFF
OCEAN
UNDERGROUND WATER

Giant waves

The largest wave ever recorded was 112 feet high. In general, the biggest waves are found around the Alguhas Current, off southern Africa. Exceptionally high "freak" waves may be preceded by an equally deep trough or "hole." Ships have been known to disappear in these.

The violent hurricane

TROPICAL cyclones can reach 350–500 miles in diameter, and move at 20–25 feet per second. They cause greatest damage in the Caribbean, Madagascar, southern Asia and the eastern coast of Australia. They destroy coastal towns and villages and underwater life. Walls of dense cloud form rings around the center of the "eye" as warm, moist air is drawn in and spirals rapidly upward. The eye itself is a relatively calm area of cool, descending air.

Tropical cyclones are called hurricanes in the Atlantic and Caribbean, typhoons in the northwest Pacific, and cyclones in the Indian Ocean. Atlantic hurricanes are given names that work through the alphabet: recent examples were Hurricane Gilbert and Hurricane Hugo.

Record breakers

Built for speed, the tea- and wool-carrying clipper ships of the last century made good use of the trade winds in their journeys between Europe and the Far East and Australia. The record was 59 days between Melbourne and England. With the opening of the Suez Canal, steamships became a more reliable method of carrying cargo around the world and the clippers gradually died out.

FORCE 12

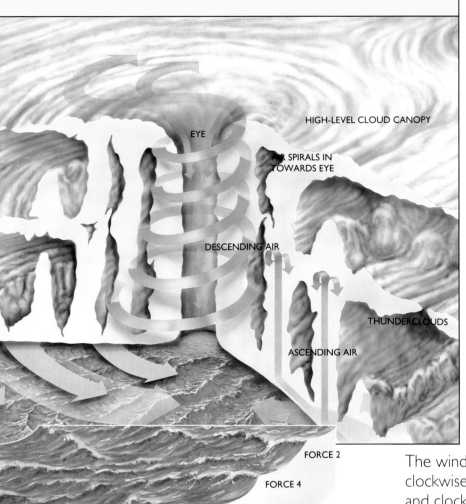

EYE

HIGH-LEVEL CLOUD CANOPY

AIR SPIRALS IN TOWARDS EYE

DESCENDING AIR

ASCENDING AIR

THUNDERCLOUDS

FORCE 2

FORCE 4

FORCE 6

FORCE 8

FORCE 10

Monsoons occur mainly in the northern Indian Ocean, the China seas and the northwestern Pacific. In summer, the land becomes hotter than the sea, and the wind blows from the ocean, usually accompanied by torrential rain. In winter, the reverse occurs.

DID YOU KNOW?

The word "ocean" comes from the Greek word "okeanos" meaning river. The early Greeks thought a river encircled the Earth.

Waterspouts are whirling masses of air, similar to tornadoes. They usually form over warm waters, when rising, warm, moist air meets cold, dry air. Immensely destructive, waterspouts can move at several feet per second and last up to 30 minutes. "Rains of fishes" appear if shoals are sucked up and then dropped further on.

The winds in cyclones blow counter-clockwise in the northern hemisphere and clockwise in the southern, and are always accompanied by torrential downpours of rain.

Most waves at sea are caused by the action of the wind on the surface. The distance from one crest to another can be over 1,000 feet and they can move at up to 60 mph. By the time they reach land, they have lost a lot of energy and are smaller. Sometimes they flatten out to form swell.

0 calm; sea like a mirror
1 light air; slight ripples
2 light breeze; small wavelets
3 gentle breeze; wave crests start to break
4 moderate breeze; small waves and some white horses
5 fresh breeze; frequent waves and many white horses
6 strong breeze; large waves 10 ft. high start
7 near gale; rough sea with spray
8 gale; waves up to 20 ft. high
9 strong gale; very high (up to 30 ft.) rough waves with much spray
10 storm; visibility difficult; waves up to 40 ft. high
11 violent storm; sea covered with foam, small ships lost to view between wave crests
12 hurricane; waves 45 ft. high and over; air filled with foam and spray.

How strong a gale?
The Beaufort Scale is used to describe the strength of the wind at sea. It is named for Francis Beaufort, an admiral in the British Navy in 1805. Although more scientific methods are now used to measure the force of the wind, this system, which relies on signs that can be seen with the eye, is still a valuable warning of stormy seas.

Wave energy
Perhaps surprisingly, water does not actually move forward with a wave. The water particles move in circles in one place; at the end of a wave the particles are back where they started. Only the energy that this generates moves forward with the wave.

11

SPRING

NEAP

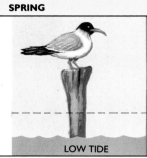
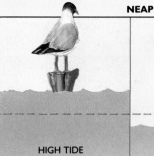

THE sun and moon exert a strong pull on the oceans and cause the tides. The moon pulls more than the sun and the tides usually follow the cycle of the moon. When the sun and moon are in line with each other and the Earth, the pull is greatest and tidal range is greatest; these are spring tides. When the sun and moon are at right angles to each other, the pull is weakest and the tidal range is small; these are neap tides.

LOW TIDE HIGH TIDE LOW TIDE

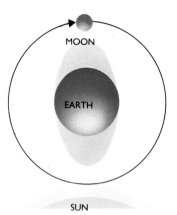
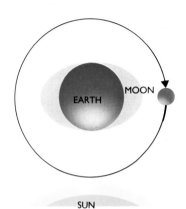

MOON

EARTH

EARTH MOON

SUN

SUN

Tidal range is the difference in height between high and low tides. The largest tidal ranges are found in bays and estuaries. On open coasts the tidal range is usually between six and ten feet. Enclosed seas, such as the Mediterranean, are almost tideless.

Tidal flows and cycles are very complex, and are affected by friction against the seafloor, the presence of land masses, and the shape of ocean basins. A diurnal tidal cycle is where there is just one high tide and one low tide a day, as in the Caribbean. On most

Ice at sea

About 12,000–15,000 icebergs are produced each year in the Arctic, most of them having broken off from Greenland glaciers. They tend to have a conical shape and often contain debris. Antarctic icebergs, on the other hand, such as the one illustrated here, break off from the ice shelf and so are often flat-topped. Tens of thousands form each year and they are much whiter than

Turtles get rid of excess salt through special glands. The secretions look like tears.

When a tide turns, the opposing currents meet and may create a whirlpool (below). One of the most violent is the maelstrom, that forms in the Lofoten Islands off northern Norway.

Salty seas

The open ocean has on average 35 parts of salt per 1,000 parts of seawater. The Red Sea is saltier (about 41 parts per 1,000) because few rivers flow into it to dilute it, and there is high evaporation in hot climates. Polar oceans are less salty because of melting glaciers.

Changes in temperature

Temperature in the ocean varies with depth (right). In the tropics there is often an abrupt temperature change, or thermocline, at around 1,000 feet. Deep cold waters cannot mix with the warm upper layers. Towards the poles, the temperatures of these layers are similar and there is no thermocline.

SECTION THROUGH INDI

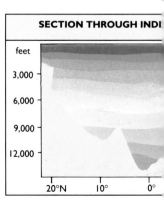

feet		
3,000		
6,000		
9,000		
12,000		
	20°N 10° 0°	

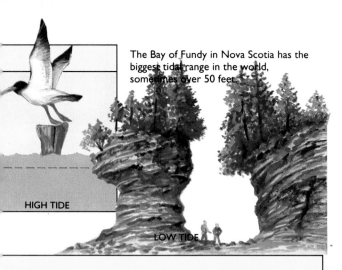

The Bay of Fundy in Nova Scotia has the biggest tidal range in the world, sometimes over 50 feet.

HIGH TIDE

LOW TIDE

Arctic icebergs. About 90 percent of an iceberg is underwater; the upper part can be over 200 feet high and several miles long.

Pack ice forms when the sea freezes. It is a major hindrance to ships. Waves and swell beneath it cause the ice to crack constantly and form floes that bump into each other, refreezing with hummocks and ridges. Usually a few channels remain open.

Atlantic coasts, there are two high and low tides and this is called a semi-diurnal tidal cycle. In parts of the Pacific and Indian oceans, tidal cycles are even more complex and are called "mixed."

The temperature of the ocean varies with depth and with latitude. In the Persian Gulf, where the sea is very shallow, temperatures can rise to 104°F. The surface waters become progressively cooler as you move away from the equator (75–85°F), to the polar oceans (32–40°F). In deeper waters, the temperature is usually very constant and is less than 40°F. Even in warm tropical waters, there are polar currents at 3,000 feet deep.

Seawater contains almost every chemical element. Some, vital to animal and plant life, occur in quite large quantities, such as sulphur, magnesium, calcium, and potassium. Iodine, which is essential to all living organisms, is concentrated in large amounts in seaweeds. There is even gold in seawater but probably not enough to make anyone rich.

ANTARCTICA

Why is the sea blue?

AS you can see when light is shone through a prism, it is made up of an array of colors. Red, orange, and yellow light are absorbed more quickly than blue light that can penetrate below a 100-foot depth. This is why clean, clear mid-ocean water looks blue on sunny days. In coastal and polar waters, the plentiful animal and plant life, as well as sediments fed by the rivers, absorb more blue light, giving the water a greenish color. This is why the color of the southern oceans around Antarctica (left) is green.

EAN

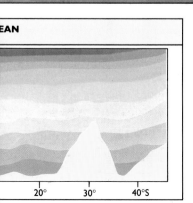

20°   30°   40°S

The stranded whales
Animals, like ships, can become trapped by pack ice. In 1989 three gray whales were stranded off Alaska. People tried to help them to escape to open water by punching holes in the ice so that they could come up to breathe. Two were eventually saved.

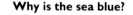

OCEAN LEGENDS

Jason and the Argonauts

Jason, the nephew of the Greek king Pelias, had to sail to the kingdom of Colchis to retrieve the Golden Fleece in order to inherit the crown. At that time, the only sailing vessels were small boats or dugout canoes. Jason, therefore, asked the giant, Argus, to build him a boat large enough for 50 men. Named the Argo, it was an enormous craft for its time. The 50 heroes and demigods who went with Jason were called the Argonauts. The Fleece was retrieved after a hazardous journey, and on his return Jason dedicated the Argo to Neptune.

Lost city of Atlantis

Atlantis was a large island or continent inhabited by warlike people who attacked Mediterranean countries. In a night of floods and earthquakes it entirely disappeared beneath the sea. Numerous places have been suggested as the lost Atlantis including Santorini, a Greek, volcanic island that suffered a massive volcanic eruption thousands of years ago, and several places in the Atlantic.

FEAR of the dangerous oceans and their cold black depths has led to widespread beliefs in sea monsters, strange beings, and supernatural phenomena at sea. These fears were compounded by the fact that little of the sea had been explored. The apparent strangeness of unfamiliar creatures brought from the depths by fishermen further fired the imagination of storytellers. Many of the stories of sea monsters are based on elements of truth. Similarly, legends of continents, such as Atlantis, lost beneath the oceans, may be based on actual places that were destroyed by real catastrophic events.

King of the sea

Neptune, who was also known as Poseidon, was the brother of Zeus, the head of the Greek gods. Neptune was king of the sea and lived in a golden palace on the seabed. He is usually shown driving over the sea in his horse-drawn chariot carrying a trident and surrounded by sea monsters. He was considered responsible for much of the weather at sea. His sons were the tritons – creatures with human bodies and fishlike tails.

Marie Celeste

The Marie Celeste was a 99-foot brig that set sail from New York in 1872 bound for Genoa with a cargo of industrial alcohol. One month later it was found drifting northeast of the Azores with only its storm sails hoisted. The captain had marked the brig's last position on the chart before leaving the boat, revealing the fact that it had sailed 600 miles alone before being found. The world's press invented numerous stories about what had happened to the crew, and it was widely but erroneously believed that when the brig was found the galley stove was still warm and there were the remains of a half-eaten meal on the captain's table. The Marie Celeste was finally wrecked on a reef off Haiti, some thirteen years later.

The kraken monster

Sea monsters are generally associated with bad luck and were often thought to be the cause of bad weather and other dangerous events at sea. The kraken was a huge monster that supposedly arose from the ocean depths to wrap its tentacles around ships. It is almost certainly based on sightings of the giant squid that can reach an immense size. In 1931 a specimen of 70 feet in length was found. The giant Pacific octopus is probably the origin of the legendary "devilfish." It can reach a length of 20 feet. Although it is docile and feeds mainly on crabs it shoots out of the water to grab birds.

The Bermuda Triangle

An area of about one million square miles lying between Bermuda, the Florida Keys, and Antigua has long been thought to have mysterious properties. It is called the Bermuda Triangle and is supposed to have claimed at least 30 aircraft and 50 ships. Explanations for these disappearances include witchcraft, reverse gravity fields, time warps, and even black holes. However, most of the losses were probably due to bad weather and hurricanes. It is now thought that the famous case of the lost squadron of U.S. Navy bombers was caused by a navigational error and that they all perished due to a lack of fuel.

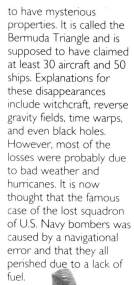

Moby Dick

Moby Dick is the most famous whale in literature. He was the creation of the American writer Herman Melville whose best known novel, called *Moby Dick*, was published in 1851. The story tells of how Captain Ahab pursues Moby Dick in his whaling boat, the *Pequod*, throughout the oceans after Moby Dick had attacked him on several occasions. Moby Dick is a "great white whale" (in fact a sperm whale) and Melville describes him as one of the greatest creatures of the sea. Moby Dick eludes capture and in the end capsizes the *Pequod*.

Mermaids

Mermaids were specifically thought to be part fish and part human. In northern countries seals were almost certainly behind the idea of mermaids. In the southern seas mermaids and mermen are considered to have white skin and to spend their time weaving. The origin of this may have been sightings of pale dugongs in sea-grass beds.

Pirates

Pirates, or robbers of the high seas, terrorized the Mediterranean at the time of the Greeks and Romans. Famous fictional pirates, such as Long John Silver from *Treasure Island*, are based on pirates in the Caribbean of the 17th and 18th centuries. Piracy is still a problem today around some isolated islands in Southeast Asia.

THE OCEAN FLOOR

THE ocean has an average depth of 1.8 miles but there are underwater chasms deeper than the highest mountains on land. Most of the seafloor consists of miles of flat plains and rolling hills, sometimes broken by mountain ridges several miles high and volcanic mountains that break the surface as islands. The complexity of the seafloor is largely explained by the fact that the Earth's crust consists of plates that move over the hot mantle material that lies beneath it.

The edges of the Atlantic and Pacific oceans are different from one another. Most of the Atlantic, and much of the Indian Ocean, has a wide continental slope with many valleys, and a pronounced continental rise. The Pacific has a mainly narrow continental shelf, 12–24 miles wide, with a steep continental slope dropping to an ocean trench, where earthquakes often occur.

Seafloor sediments
Much of the seabed is made of sands or gravels, called oozes, which were deposited thousands of years ago by rivers or coastal erosion, and from the skeletal remains of marine animals and plants. The Atlantic receives huge quantities of sediments from rivers like the Amazon, Congo, and Niger, and the oozes are up to 1,600 feet thick.

NEWFOUNDLAND

UNITED STATES

CONTINENTAL SHELF

CONTINENTAL SLOPE

CONTINENTAL RISE

MID-ATLANTIC RIDGE

PUERTO RICAN TRENCH

CUBA

PUERTO RICO

JAMAICA

HISPANIOLA

The ocean shoulders
The continental shelf is a comparatively shallow extension of the land, sloping to a depth of about 650 feet. It is the part of the ocean in which most life is found. Falling off from the shelf to the ocean floor is the continental slope. The gradient is most gentle seaward of deltas, where large amounts of sediment pour out. The continental rise is formed at the bottom of the slope by all the sediment that rolls down.

Plate boundaries
Ocean trenches are long, narrow, very deep valleys found near the edge of continents or close to island chains. They are also called "subduction zones" and are formed where one plate slides under another.

Ocean ridges are long ranges rising 0.5–2.5 miles above the sea floor. They are formed where two plates pull apart and new sea floor wells up at the ridge crest and spreads away on either side.

Exploring the deep

Much of the seafloor is still a mystery to us and has never been explored. We can get some information about it from the surface, using echo sounding and other techniques, but the most exciting discoveries have been made by manned submersibles. *Alvin* is a U.S. Navy submersible which can carry two people to depths of about 13,000 feet. It has been used to photograph the extraordinary animal communities that live around thermal vents.

Creatures of the vents

Thermal vents are like "oases" in the deep oceans. While much of the deep seabed is like a "desert" with little or no life, a wide variety of strange animals cluster around the hot springs. They occur mainly near the ocean ridges and release sulphur-rich hot water through high chimneys, known as "smokers." Worms up to ten feet long and four inches in diameter have been found living in intertwined white tubes. There are also clams ten inches long, strange limpets, crabs, sea anemones, and some fish. These animals do not need sunlight, and there are no plants for them to eat, but they make their own food, using sulphur and bacteria. Each vent may last only about 100 years, but new ones seem to form as old ones disappear.

ABYSSAL PLAIN

AFRICA

Volcanic islands

Oceanic islands are formed by volcanoes which break the ocean surface. Some are grouped in chains and linked by submarine ridges of lava. Although many volcanoes do not reach the ocean surface, some, like Maura Loa, one of the Hawaiian islands in the Pacific, are higher than Mount Everest.

Undersea plains

The abyssal plains are among the flattest places on Earth. They are formed by the sediments which rain down from the ocean surface or pour down the continental slope, smoothing the contours of the ocean crust. The Indian and Atlantic Oceans have more abyssal plains than the Pacific as they receive more sediment.

The continents and ocean basins are not fixed into position on the Earth. Although we cannot feel it, they are constantly moving at speeds of just a few inches a year. The way in which the surface of the Earth moves has been worked out in the theory of plate tectonics.

The rigid outer layer of the Earth, called the lithosphere, varies in thickness from a few miles to 150 miles and is broken into six main plates. The energy produced by heat in the deep inner part of the Earth makes the plates move over the hot, molten inner layer called the asthenosphere. The outer part of the lithosphere is called the crust.

Continental movements

THE continents of today bear little resemblance to those of 600 million years ago in the Precambrian period when a single huge continent extended from the equator to the South Pole. By about 443 million years ago this lay right over the South Pole, and was called Gondwana. By 300 million years ago, there was a new arrangement, with Gondwana having moved north to join other land masses to form Pangaea. Around 160 million years ago Pangaea broke into two main blocks: Gondwana in the south consisted of modern South America, Africa, India, Australia, and perhaps, Antarctica. Laurasia in the north was made up of what is now North America, Europe, and Asia. They were separated by the Tethys Ocean. About 100 million years ago, the Atlantic started to form as the African and South American plates moved apart, and Laurasia split into two. The Tethys Ocean was closed as India separated and moved north about 80 million years ago. The breakup of

TODAY

Gondwana was complete when Australia broke off Antarctica about 40 million years ago. The coastlines of the continents today can be fitted together like a jigsaw to show how they were originally joined up.

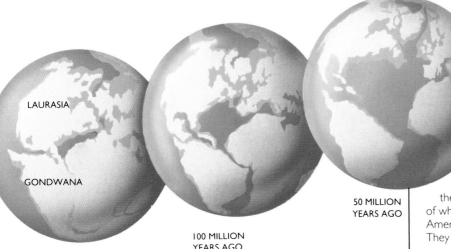

LAURASIA

GONDWANA

160 MILLION
YEARS AGO

100 MILLION
YEARS AGO

50 MILLION
YEARS AGO

NORTH
AMERICAN PLATE

PACIFIC
PLATE

NAZCA
PLATE

SOUTH
AMERICAN
PLATE

EURASIAN PLATE

AFRICAN
PLATE

INDIAN
PLATE

Shaping the ocean floor

WHERE two plates are being pushed apart, the hot material from the inner mantle rises to fill the space and form a new seafloor. Oceanic ridges form along these lines. The Pacific and Nazca plates that make up the Pacific floor are being pushed apart at the fastest rate of all plates, by about five and a half inches a year.

Where two plates are colliding, one is forced under the other and down into the mantle. This is called a subduction zone and it is here that ocean trenches are formed. These areas are usually seismic, with a high likelihood of earthquakes. Earthquakes are also common where two plates grind past each other, as is happening at the San Andreas Fault along the western coast of North America.

CONTINENTAL
CRUST

SUBDUCTION ZONE

OCEANIC RIDGE

OCEAN

MANTLE

HOT
SPOT

OUTER CORE

Birth of an ocean

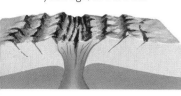

THE Red Sea may one day become an ocean. The African and Arabian plates started moving apart 70 million years ago, and are still doing so by about half an inch a year. This movement probably created the Great Rift Valley, a gash in the continental crust that runs from the Jordan Valley and Dead Sea in the north down through East Africa in the south. When this valley broke through it linked the Red Sea to the Mediterranean.

This link has been broken and rejoined several times. Once the Red Sea was connected naturally to the Mediterranean and Indian Ocean.

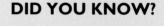

RED SEA

OCEANIC RIDGE

Oceanic crust that forms the bottoms of the ocean basins is made of basalt. Continental crust is made of granite that is less dense than basalt, and so sits on top. Oceans form, grow, shrink, or disappear depending on the relative movements of these plates. The Atlantic Ocean, for example, has probably widened by about 50 feet in the last 500 years.

Death of an ocean

The Tethys Ocean was squeezed out when the Indian plate collided with, and was subducted under, the Eurasian plate. When the continental crust of India met that of Asia it buckled up and the Himalayas were formed. Parts of the shallow continental shelf of the Tethys Ocean were lifted in the process so that marine shells can now be found thousands of feet up in the Himalayas.

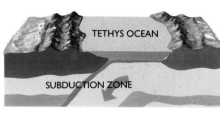

TETHYS OCEAN

SUBDUCTION ZONE

HIMALAYAS

How islands are formed

SOME islands are formed from bits of granite crust that have broken off a continent and been left behind, such as the Seychelles that were part of Gondwana 100 million years ago. Others are formed by volcanic eruptions on oceanic ridges, along subduction zones, or over hot spots.

Hot spots are where plumes of magma rise to the surface from the mantle. The hot spot is stationary and a chain of volcanoes is formed as the plate moves over it.

Sixteen hot spots are known, including the Hawaiian archipelago and Society Islands. Midway is the oldest of the Hawaiian islands and is furthest from the hot spot.

MIDWAY

HAWAIIAN ARCHIPELAGO

HAWAII

VOLCANIC ISLAND

FRINGING CORAL REEF

BARRIER REEF

ATOLL

LAGOON

Volcanic oceanic islands often develop into atolls if they are in warm regions. A fringing coral reef first grows around the island, and as the island sinks the reef keeps growing. Eventually the central island may disappear leaving a lagoon surrounded by a coral reef.

DID YOU KNOW?

Tidal waves have little connection with tides. They are usually caused by undersea volcanic eruptions or earthquakes that cause mass water movements and large waves.

Pillow lava is formed when a volcanic eruption takes place under water. As the lava is cooled rapidly by the water, it forms strange rounded shapes (above).

Islands often have unique animals and plants. Continental islands have species that may be strange descendants of those that existed on the mainland thousands of years ago, such as the sea coconut of the Seychelles (below). Species can only reach oceanic islands by wind, ocean currents, on objects such as floating logs, or by people.

SEA COCONUT

Submarines

On the ocean surface, a submarine's ballast tanks are full of air. When it dives, the valves on these tanks are opened, air rushes out, and water floods in through the ports in the bottom. To surface, high-pressure air is released into the tops of the tanks and the water is forced out (see diagram below). Conventional submarines use diesel engines when running just below the surface and battery power at greater depths.

A nuclear-powered submarine can operate for months without refueling. Oxygen and fresh water are extracted from seawater for the crew. The world's first nuclear-powered submarine, the USS Nautilus, built in 1954, achieved fame when it crossed the North Pole under the ice.

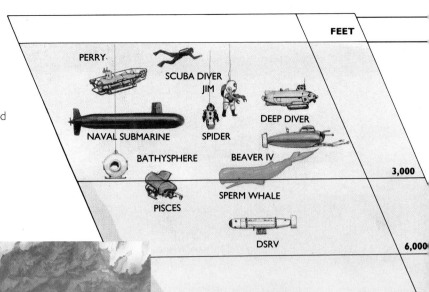

FEET

PERRY

SCUBA DIVER

JIM

DEEP DIVER

NAVAL SUBMARINE

SPIDER

BATHYSPHERE

BEAVER IV

PISCES

SPERM WHALE

3,000

DSRV

6,000

DIVING SAUCER

WRECK OF TITANIC

ALVIN

FNRS-3

JASON

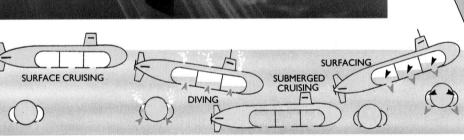

SURFACE CRUISING

DIVING

SUBMERGED CRUISING

SURFACING

Over 98 percent of the seabed is still unexplored, but in recent years enormous progress has been made in developing methods for studying the oceans. Research vessels still play an important role. Much can be learned by towing instruments behind ships, collecting samples in nets, and bringing material up from the seabed. Offshore buoys relay information by radio, and satellites can transmit readings, such as temperature, ice cover, and wave height, back to Earth.

Small, maneuverable submersibles are best suited for research and industrial purposes, and the needs of the offshore oil industry have stimulated their development. Jacques Cousteau

The voyages of Challenger

Between 1872 and 1876 the ship Challenger made deep-sea investigations at over 300 spots in all the oceans. Depth soundings were made and samples of sediment and water and specimens of plants and animals and temperature readings were taken. The equipment used by Challenger would seem very old-fashioned to modern oceanographers, but the information it gathered provided the basis for much of our knowledge about the sea.

Deep-sea diving

IDEALLY, undersea craft should have a strong hull to withstand pressure, a means of controlling buoyancy and depth, and a propulsion system.

The bathysphere was a heavy steel sphere that could be lowered from a ship's cable. In the 1930s it reached what were then record levels of around 3,000 feet. A bathyscaphe, such as *FNRS-3*, had a motor, used gasoline for buoyancy, and jettisoned iron shot when it needed to surface. In 1960 the three-man bathyscaphe *Trieste* managed to reach the bottom of the Challenger Deep, at 37,000 feet the deepest point in the sea.

Submersibles, such as *Beaver IV*, are built of very light material for buoyancy. *Pisces* is a commercial submersible that can go to 6,500 feet. Some, such as *Perry* and *Deep Diver,* have a "lock-out chamber" through which divers can leave to explore.

Jason is an ROV that explores wrecks with the help of remotely operated video cameras. The manned DSRV, or Deep Submergence Rescue Vehicle, is used to rescue sunken submarine crews.

built the first submersible, the *Soucoupe Plongeante* (diving saucer), in 1959. Submersibles consist of a pressure-proof hull, viewing ports, external lights, and a variety of manipulators, cameras, and other gadgets. Equally useful are underwater robots or ROVs (Remotely Operated Vehicles) that are usually tethered to ships from which control signals are relayed. Submersibles and ROVs are used for pipe laying, repair work, taking photos, collecting samples, launching divers at depth, and many other deep-water operations.

Diving suits

RIGID suits, such as *Spider (below)* and *Jim (see chart, center),* are like mini-submersibles and enable divers to go deeper by keeping them at surface pressure. *Spider* has its own air supply and moves with propellers driven by electric motors.

Alvin, built in 1964, is a three-man submersible that was used to explore the wreck of the Titanic. It has made more than 1,700 dives and proved invaluable in geologic and biologic studies during descents as deep as 13,000 feet.

18,000

21,000

24,000

27,000

30,000

TRIESTE

IN the 17th century, people went underwater using diving bells, and it was not until the 19th century that the "hard-hat" suit was invented. This consisted of a copper helmet and weighted boots, with air supplied from the surface. In 1943 diving was revolutionized when French marine explorer Jacques Cousteau and engineer Emile Gagnan invented SCUBA gear (Self-Contained Underwater Breathing Apparatus). Compressed air is supplied from a tank on the diver's back. Commercial divers have all sorts of gadgets to make their work easier; their suits can be heated and they use battery operated scooters to get around more quickly.

THE LIVING OCEANS

THE sea is an ideal environment for plant and animal life. It allows light to penetrate and there is abundant oxygen and many of the vital chemicals and compounds necessary for life. Its high density enables animals to float, so the largest animals on Earth have been able to live here.

Most sea life is found along coasts and in the surface waters where there is more light and food. "Pelagic" animals are those that live in the water itself. They may drift in ocean currents, like plankton, or swim, like whales. "Benthic" animals live on the sea bottom. Many, such as corals, live attached to the seabed or to other hard objects. Others live buried in sediments, like worms, or are more active and hunt, like lobsters.

GIANT SPIDER CRAB

BUTTERFLYFISH

PRAWN

HELMET SHELL

INDIAN OCEAN

PARROTFISH

WEDDELL SEAL

KELP

BLADDER WRACK

SEA LETTUCE

CORALLINA

Indian Ocean life
The Indian Ocean has many animals in common with the Pacific because they have been linked for a long time. The Red Sea, in contrast, has some unique species, including some reef fish, as it has been separated from the Indian Ocean. Much of the Indian Ocean is now a sanctuary for whales.

Marine plants
Although they are microscopic in size, the phytoplankton that floats in surface waters makes up about 90 percent of ocean plants. The others are the much larger nonflowering seaweeds (or algae) and the only flowering plants that can grow in seawater, the sea grasses.

Seaweeds are classified by their color. Brown and most green seaweeds need direct sunlight and live in shallow waters. Many of the reds and a few greens need only a little light and are found deeper or in caves. Like land plants, seaweeds are often seasonal, growing in great abundance in the spring and summer and dying off in the winter. Many seaweeds have a jelly-like texture and some have limy skeletons and look like rocks.

Antarctic life
The Southern or Antarctic Ocean has enormous numbers of marine animals that live on the abundant plankton, such as the tiny krill. Huge colonies of penguins, albatrosses, and seals are found on Antarctic shores.

Arctic life
Arctic animals are adapted to life on floating pack ice, and long cold winters. Large mammals such as the narwhal, polar bear, and seals take advantage of the abundant fish. Auks are the northern equivalent of penguins.

Atlantic life
The Atlantic has a smaller number of species than the Pacific but they are just as varied. Warm-water species like sea turtles are found in the Caribbean. Squid fishing is a major industry around the Falkland Islands. The Mediterranean has several unique plants and animals such as the beautiful and precious red coral.

ARCTIC OCEAN

NARWHAL

POLAR BEAR

AUK

COMMON DOLPHIN

BEARDED SEAL

MANATEE

RED CORAL

GIANT OCTOPUS

GIANT CLAM

MARINE IGUANA

PACIFIC OCEAN

WHITE PELICAN

GREAT WHITE SHARK

SQUID

ATLANTIC OCEAN

PENGUIN

ANGLERFISH

ALBATROSS

Albatrosses have enormous wings, enabling them to glide for hour after hour over the southern seas. The wandering albatross has a wingspan of 12 feet.

Pacific life
Animals of the Pacific range from the giant spider crab and giant octopus found in the north, to the giant clams and varied fish life found on coral reefs around atolls. Pacific islanders depend on many of the fish, mollusks, and crustaceans in these waters for food.

23

EARLIEST LIFE

It was in the ancient seas, rather than on land, that life first formed about 3,500 million years ago. One of the earliest forms of life was a microscopic organism similar to a plant that made its food using energy from sunlight and hydrogen from water. Its living descendants are known as "blue-greens" or cyanobacteria. Some blue-greens secrete lime and form stony cushions called stromatolites. Fossil stromatolites are found in many places; the oldest ones, and thus the oldest known life on Earth, are at a place called North Pole in Australia. Living ones still survive in a few places such as Shark Bay in Western Australia. The blue-greens were important because in removing hydrogen from water, they released oxygen. Gradually the concentration of oxygen in the atmosphere increased, giving us the air on which we now depend.

The first oceans

After the Earth condensed from the mass of gas and dust swirling in space, gases such as water vapor emerged from the Earth in volcanic eruptions. Water from volcanoes and rain from the sky formed ponds that gradually expanded and joined to form the first oceans and seas, four billion years ago.

Most of the Precambrian animals (inset, right) found in the earliest seas between 3,500 and 590 million years ago were soft-bodied and a little like our modern jellyfish, sea pens, and worms.

The first fish on land

COELACANTHS were the first fish to pull themselves out of the sea onto land and so were probably the ancestors of many land animals. Many species of coelacanth have been found as fossils but there is only one species still living today.

In 1938 a living coelacanth was caught off South Africa. This caused immense excitement, and since then several dozen more have been caught, mainly from around the Comoros Islands in the Indian Ocean. So many people have been trying to catch coelacanths to put on display it is feared the species could become extinct. However, it is now protected. Fortunately, the modern coelacanth lives in deep waters and unlike its fossil ancestors never tries to come on land, where it would almost certainly meet an unhappy end at the hands of collectors.

COELACANTH FOSSIL

Early seabirds

Seabirds looking much like some of those found today were living about 70 million years ago in the shallow seas that covered much of what is now North America. *Hesperornis* was flightless but swam by kicking its large webbed feet and could chase fast-moving fish underwater, catching them in its toothed beak.

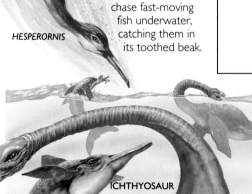

HESPERORNIS

ICHTHYOSAUR

PLESIOSAUR

Dinosaurs of the sea

The true dinosaurs all lived on land but some groups of prehistoric reptiles living about 200 million years ago took to the sea. Ichthyosaurs had dolphin-shaped bodies and plesiosaurs had long necks that were useful for catching fish. Plesiosaurs could be nearly 50 feet long and were able to come onto land on their four paddle-shaped limbs. The limbs of both ichthyosaurs and plesiosaurs were adapted as paddles for swimming and both reptiles fed on fish and squid.

Burgess shale fossils

ALTHOUGH there is a poor fossil record for most of the ancient seas, fossils were found in 1909 at Burgess Pass in British Columbia, Canada. The outcrop of shale there is formed from compressed muds laid down on the ocean edge almost 550 million years ago. Within it are preserved a variety of life forms which existed then. These fossils are some of the most perfectly preserved in the world. Many of the forms found as fossils have descendants we can recognize now, a few billion generations later, on modern beaches and sea floors, or swimming in the oceans. These include sea urchins, jellyfish, starfish, and worms.

Ammonites and trilobites

Ammonite shells were divided into air-filled compartments that made them buoyant. Some species were as big as truck wheels yet may still have been almost weightless in the water. Their only living descendant is the pearly nautilus. Trilobites had protective shells and could roll up into a ball. The only similar modern animal is the horseshoe crab.

Grand Canyon fossils

As seas have risen and fallen, and new land masses have formed, so fossils of ancient sea creatures have come to lie far inland. At the Grand Canyon in North America, the Colorado River has cut through layers of sediments that were once the bottoms of seas. About halfway down the Canyon's sides, there are 400-million-year-old fish fossils. Farther down, there are 500-million-year-old shells and worms .

The ancient seas contained more types of animal than we will ever know because many of them were largely soft-bodied and have not been preserved as fossils. About 570 million years ago there was a huge explosion of marine life, ammonites, and trilobites. However, they and hundreds of other marine species, died out inexplicably between 100 and 65 million years ago, at the same time as the dinosaurs.

Fossils form much more easily in the sea than on land because sediments are constantly laid down rather than eroded away. Dead organisms are rapidly covered and preserved.

AMMONITE

TRILOBITE

LEVELS OF OCEAN LIFE

The ocean food cycle

During winter in the northern oceans storms and currents stir up the seabed and bring nutrients (the vital elements that living organisms need) to the surface. This, combined with the extra sunlight from longer days, causes plankton to bloom and increase rapidly during spring. Once summer is over, the plankton that is not eaten by other sea creatures dies and sinks to the bottom and the whole cycle starts again. In the southern oceans the seabed is constantly stirred up and plankton is abundant throughout most of the year. Because of the thermocline (see page 12) there is little stirring in the tropics except in the upwelling areas, and so there is often less plankton.

FRIGATE BIRD

GANNET

FLYING FISH

MANGROVE TREES

TOOTHED WRACK

BASKING SHARK

COCKLE

MINKE WHALE

PLAICE

GRAY SEAL

KELP

COD

MUDSKIPPER

QUEEN SCALLOP

OCTOPUS

LUMP SUCKER

SHORE CRAB

PERIWINKLE

SAND GAPER

CONGER EEL

SEA GRASS

SEA SQUIRTS

HERMIT CRAB IN WHELK SHELL

BLUE SHARK

SEA URCHIN

EAGLE RAY

CUTTLEFISH

SEA CUCUMBER

BRITTLE STARS

RAT-TAIL FISHES

SEA PENS

SCALE WORM

HATCHET FISH

SEA LILY

CORAL

STARFISH

In shallow waters

The highest density of life on the seabed is found in shallow water down to about 300 feet. Plants such as sea grasses, kelp, and other seaweeds are found only here. Muddy and silty sea bottoms have a rich invertebrate life that attracts large numbers of seabirds. Sea cucumbers, starfish, and snail-like mollusks are found on sandy and muddy sea bottoms. Bottom-living fish are often well camouflaged.

Upper continental slopes

The types of animal found on the upper continental slope, down to 5,000 feet, depend on whether the seabed is rocky, muddy, or sandy. So that they do not sink, animals living on muds and oozes have spines, stalks, long legs, or hairs. Sea pens, for example, were named when people wrote with quills because they looked just like feathers. Sponges, corals, rays, and a variety of other fish are also found here.

Lower continental slopes and abyssal plains

The lower continental slope from 5,000 to 10,000 feet has few animals. These include worms, bivalves, sea cucumbers, and some fish that feed mainly on the remains of plants and animals that have fallen from the surface. Some species are entirely dependent on bacteria in the sediments. Tripod fish, found from 1,000 to 20,000 feet, are typical of the fish at these depths. They rest on soft oozes on their stiffened fins and tails, facing the current and trapping the rain of particles from the surface.

Similar animals are found on the abyssal plains of ooze and mud at 10,000 to 20,000 feet. The communities of animals (see page 17) found around hydrothermal vents are like oases in a desert and do not depend upon the complex food web that relies on surface-water phytoplankton.

Food for many

In healthy seas, phytoplankton is eaten almost as fast as it is produced. Numerous animals including jellyfish, comb jellies, shrimps (*Penaeus*), herrings, anchovies, and even huge blue and gray whales feed on both plant and animal plankton.

Plankton and the food web

PLANKTON, the tiny plants and animals that drift in the sunlit surface waters, are at the top of the ocean food web. Most are various types of plant or "phytoplankton" (*below*). Phytoplankton are usually found in water 100–130 feet deep. Like plants on land, these use the energy of sunlight to make food from carbon and other elements in the water, a process called photosynthesis. Diatoms are very common phytoplankton and have shells of silica. Two possible fates await all types of plankton. Either they may be eaten by larger predators, such as fish, or they may die and sink to the seabed.

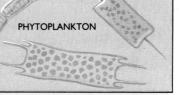

PHYTOPLANKTON

Animal plankton

The animal plankton or "zooplankton" feed on the phytoplankton. Some, such as copepods and krill, spend all their lives in the ocean surface waters. Copepods are the most abundant. Other zooplankton are the young or "larvae" of much larger marine animals such as corals and fish, many of which are eaten before they reach adulthood.

JELLYFISH

ZOOPLANKTON

Below the surface

Plankton-eaters, as well as animals that feed on them, are found in both surface waters and at depths below 300 feet. They include tuna, mackerel, sharks, and squid. The food web becomes very complicated, with larger fish, seals, whales, and seabirds eating smaller fish. Whales and seals in the southern oceans may get through 10 million tons of squid a year. Below 600 feet there is no light, and the amount of food available drops off rapidly towards 6,500 feet. At these depths predatory fish, such as hatchet fish and bristle mouths, that eat fish, squid, and crustaceans, predominate. These predators often have huge mouths and big eyes to ensure they catch any food that appears. Many also have luminous organs to attract their prey.

GRAY'S WHALE

TUNA

MACKEREL

HERRING

OAR FISH

ANGLERFISH

OPISTHOPROCTUS SOLEATUS

SPONGES

GULPER EEL

PHOTICHTHYS ARGENTEUS

TRIPOD FISH

AMPHIPODS AND ISOPODS

Ocean trenches

Surprisingly, animals have been found in deep ocean trenches that go below 20,000 feet. Each trench has its own unique community of strange and often quite large sea cucumbers, mollusks, worms, and crustaceans.

EEL

SEA CUCUMBER

WORM   LINGULA

27

INVERTEBRATES

Christmas tree worm
Many marine worms spend all their lives in tubes, catching food from the water with their feathery tentacles. Usually they can pull their tentacles back into the tube in a split second. The Christmas tree worms are brightly colored and live in tubes buried in corals.

About 97 percent of the animals in the world are invertebrates. These are animals without backbones or internal skeletons. They include many terrestrial animals, such as insects and spiders, but there is also a huge variety in the sea. They range in size from the tiny animals that float in the plankton to the huge giant squid, up to 65 feet long.

The main groups of marine invertebrates are very different from each other. Sponges, corals, and sea anemones are unable to move and live attached to rocks or the seabed.

Feather stars or crinoids are common in the tropics. They grip rocks or corals with their spiky "cirri" and use their feathery arms for swimming and filtering food from the water. They are related to starfish.

Sponges

MOST people think of sponges as something you use for washing or bathing. In fact, they are marine animals — of the simplest kind. They are basically just a collection of cells surrounding a network of holes and channels through which water flows. These nooks and crannies often provide a home for other animals such as starfish and little crabs — several thousand shrimp have been found inside a single sponge! Bath sponges all have rather dull colors, but many other sponges have brilliant colors and strange shapes. Their bodies are often supported by spicules, tiny, needle-like slivers of glass which are almost invisible. The giant vase sponges (below) found on coral reefs can grow as high as a diver. Perhaps the most amazing thing about sponges is that new sponges can grow from tiny pieces of broken sponge.

The deadly cone shell
Cone shells, like this textile cone (above) have beautifully patterned shells. They can catch fish and other animals several times their size. They spear their prey with a harpoon-like tooth and paralyze it with a nerve poison before devouring it. The poison is so powerful it can even kill human beings.

Portuguese man-of-war
Jellyfish are well named — even the firmest ones are 94 percent water. They catch food with their tentacles which are armed with stinging cells. The Portuguese man-of-war is not a true jellyfish; it is in fact a colony of similar animals that float together on the surface attached to a gas-filled sac. The tentacles can be several feet in length and are highly poisonous.

The pen shell
The pen shell is the largest Mediterranean bivalve. It is attached to the sea bottom by strong threads. In Italy the threads were once woven to make gloves.

The torpedo-shaped squid is the fastest marine invertebrate. Some species can shoot out of the water and reach speeds of up to 15 mph. Both squid and octopus produce a dark brown ink called sepia which they squirt out to confuse predators. Some deep-sea squid are luminescent (they give out light).

Scallops
Unlike many bivalve mollusks, scallops can move very quickly. They hop across the sea bed by jet propulsion, snapping their hinged shells together to shoot out a water current. They have eyes around the edge of their shells.

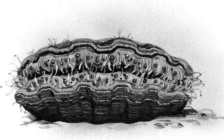

DID YOU KNOW?

Sea anemones and jellyfish are very closely related. The sea anemone is like an upside-down jellyfish that spends its life attached to rocks.

Sea urchins have a hard outer covering with many spines. They have a unique kind of mouth, called Aristotle's lantern, which has teeth to scrape algae off corals and rocks.

The sea mouse is actually a worm covered with silky bristles.

The Mediterranean murex produces a secretion which is colorless at first, but turns deep purple in sunlight. The Romans used this as a dye for their togas. No one knows what the murex uses it for!

The beautiful pirates

SEA slugs have no shell and are often poisonous, to protect them from predators. They are some of the most beautifully colored of all sea invertebrates. Their bright colors serve as a warning, or act as camouflage on the colorful coral reef. The delicate, patterned tentacles on their backs are their gills. Many sea slugs float near the surface of the water and feed on anemones and jellyfish, "pirating" the stinging cells of their prey. These are reused in the gill tufts as protection.

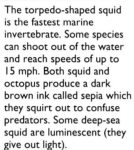

Marine worms are much more colorful than land worms and often have tentacles or bristles. The mollusks are the largest group, and include snail-like animals with a single shell, the bivalves with two hinged shells, and the octopus, squid, and sea slugs, most of which have lost their shells. The crustaceans have hard outer "suits of armor" which they have to moult in order to grow. The starfish, feather stars and sea urchins belong to a group of circular or star-shaped animals.

Life on a whale's head
Barnacles are crustaceans that live in a shell. They wave their legs outside the shell to catch food. They spend all their lives attached to rocks, man-made objects such as ships and harbor walls, and even living animals such as whales.

Hermits of the sea
Hermit crabs have soft bodies and live inside mollusk shells for protection. They change the shell as they grow. Sometimes they put other animals, such as sponges or sea anemones, onto their shells to camouflage them.

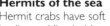

FISH

Fish include some of the ugliest and some of the most beautiful sea creatures. They range in size from large sharks to tiny colorful reef fish, but they generally have the characteristic fin and tail shape that is so well-adapted for swimming. Like marine invertebrates, they spend their entire lives underwater and obtain oxygen by passing water through their gills.

Sharks, rays, and skates have cartilaginous skeletons, and their skin is covered by tiny rough teeth called denticles.

Schools of fish

Many fish of the open sea swim together in schools, moving simultaneously in the same direction. This confuses predators, who find it difficult to follow a single individual. Schools, or shoals of fish, can be enormous. Many open-sea fish are dark on their upper parts and pale underneath. This provides camouflage from both above and below.

Hunter and hunted

THE swordfish is found in all tropical oceans but has been known to stray as far north as Iceland. The sword is in fact an elongated snout and is covered with rough tooth-like projections. It is usually a solitary hunter, using its sword to slash at shoals of fish so that it can then feed on the injured. Swordfish have been known to go right through the bottom of boats, and even pierce whales. It is not known if these are intentional attacks, or simply collisions, as they are one of the fastest creatures in the sea and can reach speeds of 150 miles per hour. They are a popular catch with sport fishermen.

Great white shark

THE great white shark has acquired a bad reputation as a result of the movies, but in fact it rarely kills humans. The great white feeds mainly on seals and porpoises and is rarely over 25 feet in length. As in all sharks, its teeth, up to three inches long, are constantly replaced. At any one time, sharks may have up to 3,000 teeth in their mouth arranged in between six and twenty rows. Only the first couple of rows are used. The others are replacement teeth that move forward on a system very similar to a conveyor belt. Great white sharks are found in warm, but usually not tropical, seas. Most have been sighted off the coasts of California and Australia.

They are usually unable to keep afloat unless they swim. Many sharks also have to keep a constant stream of water passing through their gills or they will drown, so they spend most of their time swimming. A few are able to pump water through their gills: these species can lie on the sea bottom. Most fish have bony skeletons and are covered with bony scales. The bony fish have a swim bladder, or air sac, that allows them to float.

Gliders of the seas

Manta rays (left) are flattened relatives of sharks and are the largest of the skates and rays. The Pacific manta has a wingspan of over 24 feet and weighs up to 3,500 lbs. It is one of the most majestic swimmers, gliding through the surface waters of the tropical oceans, flapping its "wings." Despite its size, it feeds on small fish and invertebrates that it filters out of the water. The two fins that project from its head like horns have given it the name "devilfish."

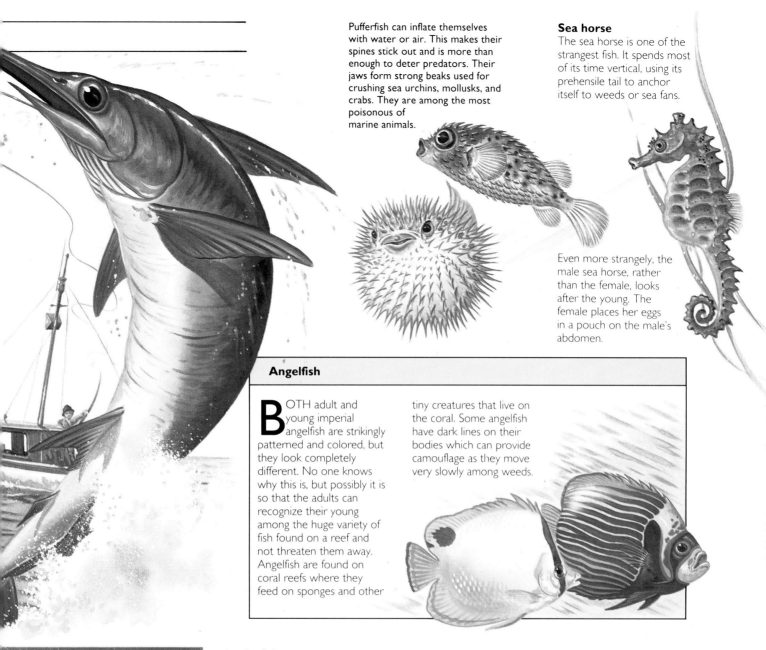

Pufferfish can inflate themselves with water or air. This makes their spines stick out and is more than enough to deter predators. Their jaws form strong beaks used for crushing sea urchins, mollusks, and crabs. They are among the most poisonous of marine animals.

Sea horse

The sea horse is one of the strangest fish. It spends most of its time vertical, using its prehensile tail to anchor itself to weeds or sea fans.

Even more strangely, the male sea horse, rather than the female, looks after the young. The female places her eggs in a pouch on the male's abdomen.

Angelfish

BOTH adult and young imperial angelfish are strikingly patterned and colored, but they look completely different. No one knows why this is, but possibly it is so that the adults can recognize their young among the huge variety of fish found on a reef and not threaten them away. Angelfish are found on coral reefs where they feed on sponges and other tiny creatures that live on the coral. Some angelfish have dark lines on their bodies which can provide camouflage as they move very slowly among weeds.

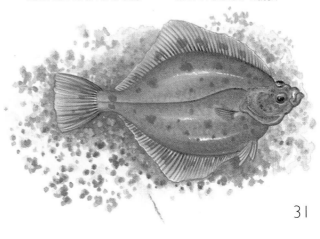

Anglerfish

Anglerfish are among the ugliest of sea creatures. They are often flabby and lumpy and usually have huge mouths. They have very elastic stomachs and tend to eat anything. Their name comes from the lure on their heads, an adaptation of one of their dorsal fin rays, with a tiny, fleshy flap at the end of it. This can be moved around like a bait on a line to attract other small fish that the anglerfish then eats. Deep-sea anglerfish (left) living in dark waters have luminous lures. The light on these lures is formed by chemicals or by bacteria that glow naturally.

Flatfish

Flatfish, such as plaice, flounders, and halibut, start life as normal-shaped fish with an eye on each side of the head. As they grow, one eye moves round and the mouth twists until the adult can lie on one side.

Adults can change color perfectly to match the pattern and color of the seabed, thus helping to protect themselves from predators. They also often bury themselves in the sand in shallow water.

31

MAMMALS

Sea otter

The sea otter of the north Pacific rarely comes ashore. It digs for clams and finds food in the kelp. Apart from monkeys and humans, it is the only animal known to use a tool. It breaks open abalone and other mollusks between two stones while floating on its back. At night, it wraps itself in giant seaweed to avoid drifting out to sea. It was hunted almost to extinction but it is now protected and populations have increased.

Unlike fish, mammals and reptiles have to come to the surface of the sea to breathe air, and most must come to shore to breed and lay their eggs. Nevertheless, they are well adapted to life underwater and their bodies are designed to conserve oxygen. When diving, a seal's heartbeat may slow from about 140 beats a minute to less than 15. Mammals have a high body temperature and lose heat more rapidly in water than in air. Most marine mammals therefore have a special layer of fat, called blubber, under the skin that provides insulation. Reptiles, which are cold-blooded, must find other ways of keeping warm. Marine iguanas bask in the sun to warm up before swimming; marine turtles solve the problem by living mainly in tropical seas. The fact that they have to come ashore to breed, and are very clumsy on land, has meant that many marine mammals and reptiles are vulnerable to hunters.

Sea snakes are found in the Indian and Pacific oceans. They have very strong venom but rarely bite humans. They may be the most abundant reptiles on Earth.

A poorly adapted mammal

HUMAN beings are very poorly adapted to life underwater. The invention of scuba gear has meant that we can get some idea of what it is like to be a seal. A diver takes compressed air down to provide oxygen. A special diving suit keeps her warm. Fins make fairly good paddles, and a mask helps her to see. But we have not solved the problem of eating under water! A diver on land in all her equipment is almost as clumsy as a seal on land.

Seals in combat

Adult seals usually gather once a year to breed, sometimes thousands crowding on to one beach at the same time. The males set up territories and fight fiercely with each other. Bull elephant seals have particularly vicious fights over their females. Their strange trunk-like noses are inflated and used to threaten other males. Bulls may be three times the weight of the females. Like other true seals (those with no external ear flaps), elephant seals have great difficulty moving on land. In contrast, eared seals can turn their hind flippers forward and move fairly quickly on land. The limbs of all seals are adapted for swimming. Eared seals, such as sea lions and fur seals, swim with their front flippers. The true seals use their hind flippers for power and their front flippers to steer.

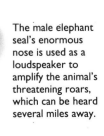

The male elephant seal's enormous nose is used as a loudspeaker to amplify the animal's threatening roars, which can be heard several miles away.

Walrus

The walrus lives in the Arctic. Its long tusks are modified teeth and are used to help it pull itself out on to ice floes and to show its dominance over other walruses. The largest animal with the largest tusks generally wins in fights. Walruses have very thick skins to protect themselves from injury in fights. Like seals, walruses may have problems keeping cool in hot sunshine. They often go pink in the sun, as the blood comes to the skin surface to cool down.

Sea cows

Surprisingly, dugongs and manatees are related to elephants rather than to seals. They live in shallow tropical waters, and like whales do not come ashore at all. Dugongs live in the Indian and Pacific oceans and feed on sea grasses, which has given rise to their common name, "sea cows." Manatees are found in the Atlantic and Caribbean, often living in coastal rivers and estuaries.

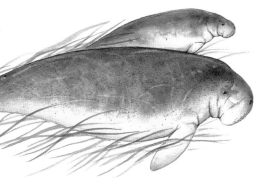

DID YOU KNOW?

The Weddell seal is one of the largest seals and holds the seal diving record. It can stay under for over an hour, and reach a depth of nearly 2,000 feet.

The polar bear eats fish, seals, and even walrus and beluga whales. It swims well, has partly webbed feet, a water-repellent coat, and a thick layer of fat.

Baby harp seals have white coats for camouflage. Later they grow dark adult coats.

Marine iguanas

MARINE iguanas are equally good at clambering around the rocky shores of the Galapagos Islands and diving to depths of up to 50 feet. The only species of lizard living in the sea, they are very good swimmers with webbed feet and tails that are flattened sideways. They feed on seaweeds. Except for the breeding season, when the males often fight over the females, these otherwise harmless creatures spend their time in large groups, sometimes even lying one on top of another, warming themselves in the sun.

Baby turtles

Turtles have large flat legs and although bulky and ungainly on land, move gracefully in the water. They can reach speeds of up to 20 miles per hour. The female lays her eggs on shore, buried in the sand. At cooler temperatures more males are born; at hotter temperatures there are more females. When the young hatch, like these hawksbill turtles, they rush down the shore to the sea. Turtles in the Gulf of Mexico hibernate on the seabed during the winter.

33

Some of the largest whales, such as the blue, gray, and right whales, have no teeth. They feed by straining small animals and plankton through horny plates of baleen that hang like curtains from the roof of the mouth. A blue whale may eat up to two and a half tons of food every day.

THE blue whale is the largest animal ever known, reaching over 100 feet in length — four times as big as any known dinosaur. It is found in all oceans but is now very rare. The Antarctic populations were only discovered this century but were quickly decimated. Over 29,000 blue whales were killed in one hunting season in the 1930s. The world population may now be down to a few thousand. Heaviside's dolphin (below) is probably the smallest cetacean, reaching just four and a half feet in length. It lives around South Africa in the Benguela current system, but little is known about it.

A whale breathes through a blowhole in the top of its head. The spout is formed by spray as the whale blows out. Toothed whales have a single blowhole. Baleen whales have two blowholes and their spout has a forked appearance.

Whales, dolphins, and porpoises are a group of mammals called cetaceans. They have streamlined bodies and were once thought to be fish. The hindlimbs have been lost and the forelimbs have become fins or flippers. They swim by thrusting their tail flukes up and down in the water, unlike fish, which move their tails from side to side. Pilot whales can reach speeds of up to 30 miles per hour. Finback whales can dive to over 1,500 feet and swim for 40 minutes without breathing.

Breaching
Many whales and dolphins breach, or leap right out of the water. This may stun or panic fish shoals, and may also be a way of communicating with each other. The humpback whale (left), weighing more than 60 tons, manages to burst into the air and do a backward somersault! Some whales can also position themselves vertically with their head out of the water, a maneuver known as "spy-hopping."

Whales have no fur and keep warm with a layer of blubber under the skin, which is up to 20 inches thick in the bowhead whale. Most whales and dolphins have teeth and eat fish, squid, and other animals. They often hunt cooperatively, herding shoals of fish together by breaching and diving.

Ending the hunt

WHALES have been hunted by humans since the time of the Vikings. The most important product was oil from the blubber, liver, and skeleton, that was used both for food and as a lubricant. The meat is also popular in some countries. The sperm whale produces a strange product in its intestine called ambergris that is used in the perfume industry. Traditionally, whales were hunted with harpoons from small boats and the carcasses were towed ashore. When factory whaling ships appeared in the 1920s, whales could be cut up and frozen on board and the harvest became more intensive. Gradually all the whales have been over-harvested.

The International Whaling Commission

This whale has been "flensed," its skin completely stripped from its body.

The sea unicorn

EARLY explorers called the narwhal the sea unicorn because of its single long tusk. This is formed by the spiral growth of the left tooth that can reach 10 feet in length. Usually, only the males have tusks. The function of the tusk is still not clear, although narwhals have been seen jousting.

Narwhals live in Arctic waters and feed on fish, shrimp, squid, and octopus.

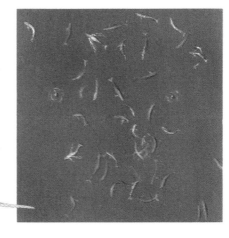

Beluga whales, white in color, congregate in huge herds in North American estuaries during the breeding season (above). Belugas are known as the canaries of the sea because of their complex songs. Belugas also use facial expressions and often seem to be "smiling."

Common dolphin
The common dolphin is well known to us as one of the friendliest and most intelligent of marine animals. Normally living in groups, or "schools," of up to a few hundred dolphins, they are among the fastest swimmers in the oceans, capable of reaching speeds of up to 25 mph.

was set up in the 1940s to regulate harvests. Thanks to campaigns such as those by Greenpeace, most commercial whaling has now ceased. However, there is still some whaling by local people for food, and many of the smaller whales and dolphins are killed accidentally in big fishing nets on the high seas.

Killer whale
Found all over the world, including the polar seas, killer whales, or orcas, are closely related to dolphins. They are the only cetaceans to feed on mammals, such as seals and porpoises, as well as on seabirds, squid, and fish. They are able to take seal pups or penguins off the beach or ice (below).

Killer whales work together in groups of up to forty animals, called pods, when hunting. They circle the shoal of fish, herd of dolphins, or perhaps a rocky islet with basking seals, and once their prey is trapped, they strike. Their name is in recognition of their hunting prowess, but killer whales rarely attack humans.

BIRDS

Wandering albatross

The wandering albatross has the largest wingspan of any bird, up to 11 feet in length. Gliders rather than fliers, they glide downwind from a height of about 50 feet and just before hitting the water turn into the wind that blows them back up again. They feed mainly on fish, crustaceans, and squid which they seize from the surface.

Plunge diver

Many seabirds, including gannets, the brown pelican, boobies, and terns, are expert "plunge divers." By diving from great heights (in the case of gannets, up to 100 feet), they build up enough momentum to reach prey well below the surface. Despite the difficulty of this fishing method, terns are often successful in one dive out of three. Their skulls are strengthened to withstand the impact against the water.

Most pelicans can be found on inland bodies of water and do not dive. The brown pelican is mainly marine. When it catches sight of a fish it plunges vertically, straightening its neck just before entering the water. Having dived, it uses its expandable bill (common to all pelicans) to scoop up a large mouthful of fish.

Only about 300 species, or three percent of the total number of different kinds of birds, live on the coast and oceans, but they make up for this by occurring in huge numbers. Enormous concentrations of seabirds are found in areas of upwelling (see page 8), such as in the Southern Ocean, and off the coasts of Peru and Chile. Some seabirds, like the albatrosses, spend almost their entire lives at sea, coming to land every other year to nest. Others, such as waders, ducks, and cormorants, are found along the shore all year round. Seabirds have a wide variety of feeding methods, from swimming underwater to catch fish, chasing other birds and forcing them to drop their prey, to plunge-diving into the sea themselves.

A guillemot bazaar

GUILLEMOTS breed on cliffs at closer densities than any other bird, often in bodily contact. There may be up to 70 pairs in three square feet, and their colonies are known as "loomeries" or "bazaars." Despite this crowding, each pair defends a tiny territory. The eggs, as with many seabirds, are laid directly on the bare rock. Their color and marking is very variable and helps the parents to recognize their own eggs. The chicks are recognized by their voices.

Eider duck

Most seabirds, and all sea ducks, have webbed feet for swimming. There are only a few true sea ducks, such as the eiders and scoters. The eider is found in large numbers in northern Europe. The female eider lines her nest with fine down feathers that she plucks from her breast. In Scandinavia the down is removed from the nests to make quilts or "eiderdowns."

Puffins

Seabirds breed in pairs, and many mate for life. Puffins lay a single egg at the ends of the burrows that they excavate with their beaks in turf on the cliffs. In larger colonies the ground can become honeycombed with burrows. The puffin's bill becomes brightly colored to help it attract a mate.

A frigate bird display

FRIGATE birds are some of the best fliers, gliding on air currents and thermals (warm upcurrents) while seldom flapping their wings. The male has a red throat pouch that is inflated during courtship. The display is one of the best among seabirds. Males display on the nest site in groups of 30, spreading and vibrating their wings when females fly overhead, throwing back their heads and clacking their bills. When a female lands beside a chosen male, the pair snake their heads and necks across each other. The name, frigate bird, refers to its habit of obtaining food by harassing other birds in flight; a frigate is a warship.

DID YOU KNOW?

Rocky islets used by seabirds become covered with a thick layer of guano, or droppings. This is rich in phosphates, and in several areas, such as off the coast of Peru, it has been mined for fertilizer.

The fairy (or white) tern lays a single egg precariously on a tree branch, without even building a nest. A single egg is easily concealed from potential predators.

Gulls are the most familiar seabirds. They feed on fish and mollusks and can be seen dropping oysters or cockles from a height to break them on rocks below before eating.

Emperor penguins

Female emperor penguins lay a single egg which is then incubated by the male for 64 days on its feet. The female returns with food for the chick after it hatches.

Penguins are the best bird swimmers. They hunt for fish underwater, using their flipper-like wings.

Seabirds may return year after year to a safe site on cliffs and isolated islands to breed. They often form very large colonies in order to protect the eggs and young from predatory gulls, crows, and other invaders. Their black-and-white plumage helps to camouflage them when they are seeking fish. Many seabirds have been heavily hunted for their meat and eggs. Their eggs are vulnerable as they are often laid on the ground.

OCEAN MIGRATIONS

Pacific salmon

Pacific salmon spend most of their lives at sea. Small salmon, or smolts, feed on plankton at first, and then on fish. When they become adults, they travel to the American coast. They find the exact river in which they were born, using their excellent sense of smell. They battle upstream, leaping up waterfalls, to the shallow pools where they were born. Here they mate, and die shortly afterwards. The eggs hatch in spring, and for a few weeks the baby salmon feed on insects and crustaceans in the stream. Then they swim downriver to the sea and start the cycle again.

MANY animals make long journeys, either every year, or at different stages of their lives. Sometimes, as for the arctic tern, this is to take advantage of different sources of food. For others, such as the gray whale, it is to find a suitable place to breed. Some use the ocean currents and winds, like young eels that float back to Europe in the Gulf Stream. Many, incredibly, do it under their own power, including the spiny lobsters that tramp along the sea bottom. Various types of navigation systems are called into use. Birds use the sun's position to estimate compass directions. Salmon use smell to find the river where they were born. Scientists have found that if they block a salmon's nostrils it will get lost.

Migrating animals were a source of wonder to early naturalists. How eels reproduce was a mystery until the end of the last century because no one ever saw a baby eel. Aristotle thought they were formed from the soil. In the 18th century people thought that they came from the hairs of horses' tails and in the 19th century it was even suggested that a beetle gave birth to eels. The reason for the puzzle was that

Gray whale

The Californian gray whale migrates each spring and fall along the west coast of North America. Its summer feeding grounds are in the shallow parts of the Bering Sea. The winter calving grounds are in the shallow lagoons of Baja California. When the calves are born, the whales return north. This is the longest migration of any mammal – a round trip of 12,700 miles every year. Its normal traveling speed on migration is 4.5 knots (5 mph) although it can reach speeds of 11 knots (12 mph). When migrating, it surfaces every three or four minutes and blows three to five times. The Korean gray whale makes a similar journey from the Okhotsk Sea off the coast of Siberia to the islands of South Korea. There used to be gray whales in the North Atlantic, but they have been hunted to extinction in this ocean.

Okhotsk Sea

Bering Sea

ARCTIC OCEAN

PACIFIC SALMON

GRAY WHALE

NORTH AMERICA

SPINY LOBST

PACIFIC OCEAN

BAJA CALIFORNIA

RANGE OF EUROPEAN EEL

ONE YEAR

TWO YEARS

THREE YEARS

FOUR YEARS

Arctic tern

Arctic terns are the greatest travelers of all. They nest in the north, sometimes north of the Arctic Circle, in the northern summer. When only a few weeks old, the chicks set off on an 11,000-mile journey south. They pass the western coasts of Europe and Africa, and travel across the Southern Ocean, to spend the southern summer on pack ice not far from the South Pole. By doing this, they take advantage of the very long summer daylight hours at both North and South poles for feeding. The arctic tern probably sees more daylight hours than any other animal.

adult eels live in fresh water, but migrate to the sea to breed. For many migratory land and shore birds, the oceans, offering them neither places to rest nor sources of food, are a major obstacle on their journey. They therefore tend to concentrate at points where the sea is narrowest in order to make the crossing. Many thousands of birds of prey, for example, cross the narrow Straits of Gibraltar in the spring and fall on their way to and from Africa and northern Europe. Some birds follow routes that avoid large open stretches of water.

Spiny lobster

Spiny lobsters move south through the Caribbean in the fall to spend winter in deeper waters. The migration happens at the onset of cold temperatures. As many as 100,000 individuals may migrate at a time, in single files of up to 60 animals. Each animal keeps in contact with the one ahead using its antennae to touch the other's abdomen. The white spots on their tails may help them keep in line. They may travel a total of 30 miles on the sea bottom.

EUROPE

AFRICA

EUROPEAN EEL

Sargasso Sea

ASCENSION ISLAND

ATLANTIC OCEAN

aribbean Sea

GREEN TURTLE

ARCTIC TERN

SOUTH AMERICA

Green turtle

The green turtle may travel thousands of miles to return to the same beach each year to lay her eggs. This is often the beach where she was born herself. Green turtles that feed off the coast of South America travel 3,000 miles every two to three years to breed on remote Ascension Island. Some green turtles make shorter coastal migrations, and a few, such as the Hawaiin population, stay in the same area all year round. Little is known about the male green turtles, but it is likely that they make similar migrations to the females.

European eel

European eels live in rivers but move down to the sea to breed. When about six years old, they travel some 4,000 miles across the Atlantic, taking between four and seven months to reach the Sargasso Sea. Here their eggs are laid in the deep, warm waters. After hatching, the young, transparent, leaf-shaped eels, called leptocephali or glass eels, drift back in the Gulf Stream, taking about three years to reach Europe. In the cooler, shallower waters they turn into young adults called elvers, and move up the rivers where they become fully grown adult eels, ready to start the cycle again.

THE OCEAN MARGINS

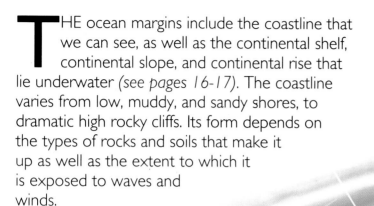

THE ocean margins include the coastline that we can see, as well as the continental shelf, continental slope, and continental rise that lie underwater *(see pages 16-17)*. The coastline varies from low, muddy, and sandy shores, to dramatic high rocky cliffs. Its form depends on the types of rocks and soils that make it up as well as the extent to which it is exposed to waves and winds.

The coastline is always changing, as some areas are eroded by waves and strong

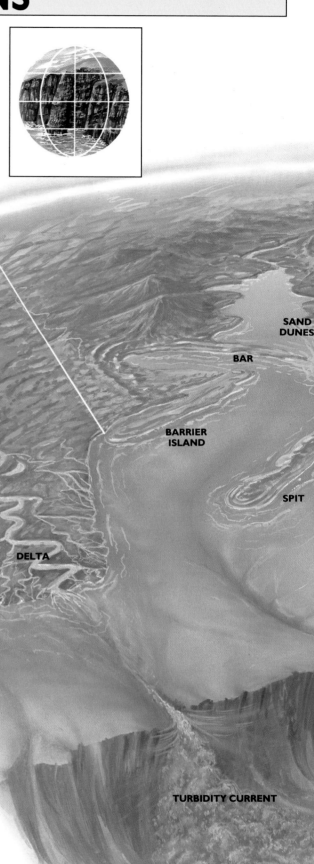

SAND
DUNES

BAR

BARRIER
ISLAND

SPIT

DELTA

TURBIDITY CURRENT

Sea levels

Sea levels are constantly changing and have a major effect on the appearance of coastlines. Since the end of the last Ice Age, sea levels have been rising slowly, but in the future they may rise much more rapidly. Human activities, such as the burning of fossil fuels, are increasing the amounts of carbon dioxide and certain other gases, known as greenhouse gases, in the atmosphere and these are causing the world to warm up. As this happens, glaciers will melt and release water into the sea, and the seawater will expand as its temp — erature increases. Any increase in sea level would be disastrous in places like Bangladesh *(left)* where much of the country is less than 15 feet above sea level and flooding is already a

BANGLADESH

0 – 100 INCH RISE

0 INCH RISE

CURRENT SEA LEVEL

RAISED BEACHES

serious problem.

The ice ages reduced sea levels as water was taken up in the expanding polar ice caps. Falling seas may leave behind "raised" beaches *(above)*, isolated above the new beach which forms below it.

Coast formations

There are several types of coast formation. Deltas are formed at the mouths of large rivers that bring down enormous quantities of sediment. They extend up to 30 miles out to sea. The Mississippi is one of the largest deltas in the world, and the sediment is thought to be six miles thick.

Spits, bars, and barrier islands are formed when sand, gravel and shingle are deposited by the tide and waves. Dunes are formed by windblown sand.

At the mouths of estuaries large mud flats are formed in sheltered areas where there is little scouring action. Marshy coasts may develop in sheltered bays where sand and mud are deposited.

tidal currents while others grow and gradually creep seaward as mud, sand, and gravel are deposited. Large waves tend to erode the coast, but small waves stabilize beaches and deposit sediment. Waves usually strike the shore at an angle, so that sediments, having been eroded in one area, are carried along and deposited in another. Sometimes changes are very dramatic and sudden, as in a storm or hurricane, when large portions of coast may be washed away. Usually changes occur slowly over many years.

MUD FLATS

ESTUARY

CLIFFS

STACK

ARCH

CONTINENTAL SHELF

CANYON

CONTINENTAL SLOPE

SEDIMENT

CONTINENTAL RISE

Rocky coasts

Rocky coasts are usually the most scenic, particularly where erosion has caused complex chasms, pinnacles, caves, and arches (above). A hole in the roof of a cave may form a blowhole which makes strange noises as air and water are forced through it.

The continental slope

The continental slope varies in gradient. Large amounts of sediment are deposited off deltas. It is often cut by deep V-shaped valleys and canyons which may have been formed by erosion in the last Ice Age and have since been widened by turbidity currents. These are underwater avalanches that occur when large amounts of sediment resting on the upper continental slope are dislodged by earthquakes or their own weight. This mass of sediment, up to several miles in length and width and several hundreds of feet thick, rolls down the slope at speeds of up to 50 mph.

41

The varied habitats found on the coast are home to a wide range of plants and animals. Coasts may be sheltered or exposed to wind and waves; they may be stony, sandy, muddy, or with cliffs. Coastal habitats also include coral lagoons, estuaries, and ice shelves. Where sand and mud is deposited in sheltered bays and estuaries, sea grasses, mangroves, and other marine plants can become established. These trap more silt and the marsh or mangrove swamp grows

A mangrove swamp

Unlike most trees, mangroves are able to tolerate salt, regular immersion in water, and the lack of oxygen in the muddy silt in which they grow. Their roots are specially adapted to obtain oxygen from the air. Some form buttresses or descend from branches as aerial roots while others protrude like little chimneys from the soil. Mangroves often have large floating seeds, that sometimes start to develop on the tree. The maze of roots traps sediment and provides a sheltered nursery for young fish and prawns. Mangroves are also a valuable source of fuelwood and timber. Despite their importance, mangroves are being destroyed worldwide and replaced with fish-farming ponds, houses, and marinas (see page 57).

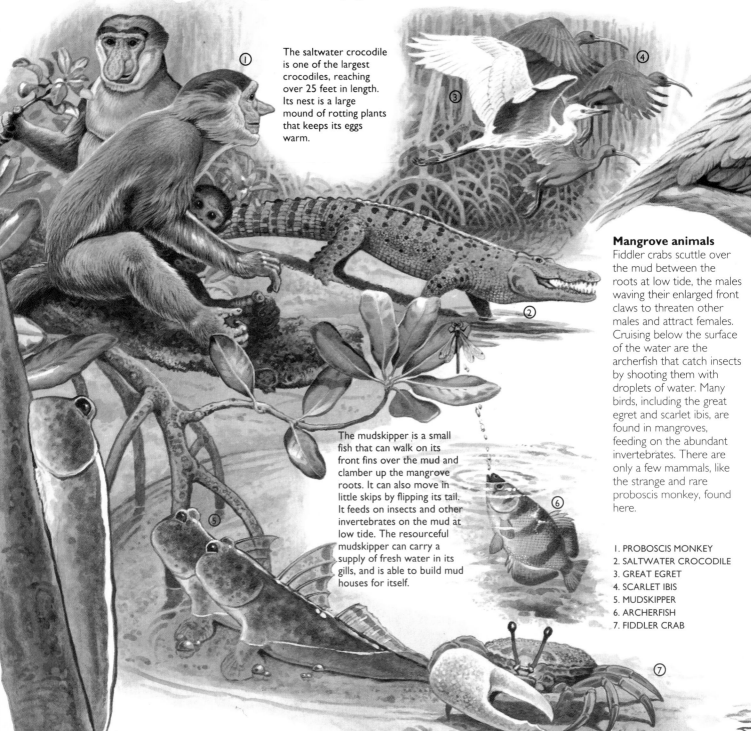

The saltwater crocodile is one of the largest crocodiles, reaching over 25 feet in length. Its nest is a large mound of rotting plants that keeps its eggs warm.

The mudskipper is a small fish that can walk on its front fins over the mud and clamber up the mangrove roots. It can also move in little skips by flipping its tail. It feeds on insects and other invertebrates on the mud at low tide. The resourceful mudskipper can carry a supply of fresh water in its gills, and is able to build mud houses for itself.

Mangrove animals

Fiddler crabs scuttle over the mud between the roots at low tide, the males waving their enlarged front claws to threaten other males and attract females. Cruising below the surface of the water are the archerfish that catch insects by shooting them with droplets of water. Many birds, including the great egret and scarlet ibis, are found in mangroves, feeding on the abundant invertebrates. There are only a few mammals, like the strange and rare proboscis monkey, found here.

1. PROBOSCIS MONKEY
2. SALTWATER CROCODILE
3. GREAT EGRET
4. SCARLET IBIS
5. MUDSKIPPER
6. ARCHERFISH
7. FIDDLER CRAB

Wading the waters

ESTUARIES, mud flats, and marshes are among the richest feeding grounds for many birds, and enormous flocks may congregate at low tides. These birds, often known as waders, have widely spaced toes that prevent them from sinking into the mud. Sandy and muddy shores often seem bare, with nothing on the surface at low tide, but hundreds of mollusks, ragworms, crustaceans, and sea urchins can be found by digging. Some waders, such as curlews, plovers, and sandpipers, are experts at this and their beaks are specially adapted. Others, like spoonbills, scoop up animals in the shallow waters.

out seaward. In tropical countries, mangroves are the main coastal vegetation. In cooler parts of the world, marshes are dominated by reeds, rushes, grasses, and other salt-tolerant plants.

The shore is "zoned" with different plants and animals found at different levels, depending on how well they can cope with salinity and total immersion. This is seen particularly well on rocky shores where, as in northern Europe, each zone even has its characteristic type of periwinkle snail.

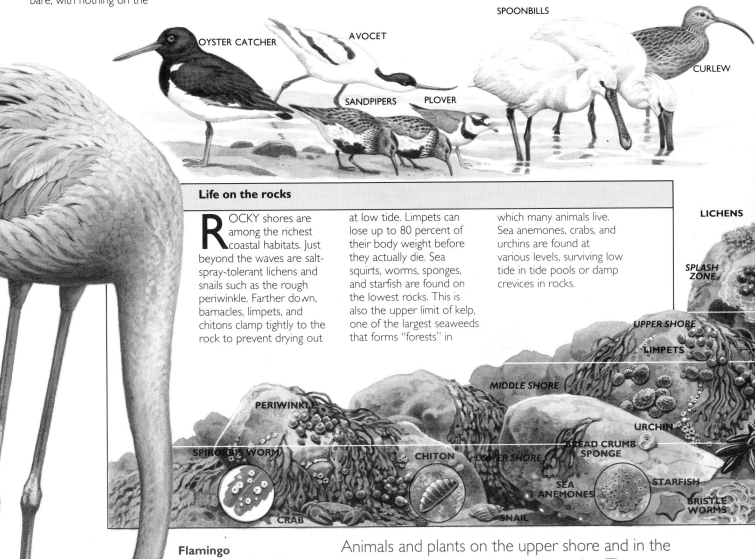

OYSTER CATCHER — AVOCET — SPOONBILLS — CURLEW — SANDPIPERS — PLOVER

Life on the rocks

ROCKY shores are among the richest coastal habitats. Just beyond the waves are salt-spray-tolerant lichens and snails such as the rough periwinkle. Farther down, barnacles, limpets, and chitons clamp tightly to the rock to prevent drying out at low tide. Limpets can lose up to 80 percent of their body weight before they actually die. Sea squirts, worms, sponges, and starfish are found on the lowest rocks. This is also the upper limit of kelp, one of the largest seaweeds that forms "forests" in which many animals live. Sea anemones, crabs, and urchins are found at various levels, surviving low tide in tide pools or damp crevices in rocks.

LICHENS — SPLASH ZONE — UPPER SHORE — LIMPETS — MIDDLE SHORE — URCHIN — PERIWINKLE — SPIRORBIS WORM — CHITON — LOWER SHORE — BREAD CRUMB SPONGE — SEA ANEMONES — STARFISH — BRISTLE WORMS — CRAB — SNAIL

Flamingo
Flamingoes are found in coastal lagoons in some parts of the world, as well as around inland lakes. The Caribbean flamingoes (left), are the most brightly colored. Their red or pink color comes from pigments that occur in the food that they eat. They feed on algae and tiny animals by pumping water through their beaks.

Animals and plants on the upper shore and in the "splash zone" are basically land species. Those on the middle shore, such as seaweeds, barnacles, and limpets, need a daily immersion in seawater. The lower shore is only uncovered at low spring tide: most animals here cannot survive out of water. In mangrove forests, different species are found as you move further inland, depending on the salinity, the amount of fresh water received from rivers, and the amount of tidal flooding.

CORAL REEFS

Types of reef

There are three main types of reef. Fringing reefs lie close to the shore along continental coasts and around islands. Barrier reefs lie at some distance from the shore. Atoll reefs, formed when a volcanic island "sinks" and the reef continues to grow, are circular and often topped with small sandy islands.

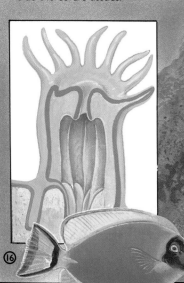

ATOLL

VOLCANO

FRINGING REEF

1. EAGLE RAY
2. MORAY EEL
3. GIANT CLAM
4. SEA URCHINS
5. SEA SLUG
6. GROUPER
7. CLEANER WRASSE
8. BRAIN CORAL
9. SEA ANEMONE
10. CLOWN FISH

11. STARFISH
12. DAMSEL FISH
13. THREAD-FIN BUTTERFLYFISH
14. SPINY LOBSTER
15. BUTTERFLY FISHES
16. SURGEONFISH
17. SOLDIERFISH
18. HAWKFISH
19. PARROTFISH
20. FLASHLIGHT FISH

Polyps

The tiny coral animals called polyps secrete a stony, cup-shaped skeleton around them. The tentacles catch food although the coral gets most of its food from tiny single-celled plants that live inside the coral's tissues.

CORAL reefs are the richest, most colorful, and varied of all marine habitats. The greatest number of reef plants and animals are found in Southeast Asia where a single reef can contain 3,000 species. Reefs mainly grow in clear, shallow, tropical waters, extending slightly farther north or south where there are warm currents, as in Florida, Japan, and Australia. A reef is constructed of coral colonies that are very varied in shape and color. Colonies are formed by tiny coral animals that divide to create new animals that lie on the skeletons of dead animals. Only the outside of a colony, therefore, has living animals on it. Brain corals grow slowly and have annual growth rings like trees. Some coral colonies have been found that are between 800 and 1,000 years old.

More species of fish can be seen on a reef than in any other habitat in the sea. They range from tiny gobies that live in crevices to large sharks that cruise along the edge of a reef looking for food. Butterfly fish are among the most colorful and are often seen in pairs. Clown fish live among the tentacles of sea anemones to protect themselves.

Spawning

Like other marine invertebrates, many corals reproduce by spawning. This means that the eggs and sperm are released into the water at the same time, where the sperm then fertilizes the egg. The baby coral that is formed is called a larva. On some reefs almost all the corals spawn on the same night of the year. On the Great Barrier Reef it happens in spring, in the week following full moon, just after dark.

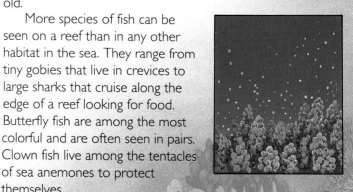

44

Mollusks are often difficult to see on a reef because they are well camouflaged and often nocturnal. Although awkward to spot, there are actually more species of mollusk than fish, with 4,000 species known from the Great Barrier Reef alone. Giant clams are an exception in that they are easily seen because of their brilliant blue mantles. On the reef there are also numerous crustaceans such as spiny lobsters and the banded cleaner shrimps that obtain food by picking parasites off fish. Sea urchins are also abundant and graze on small algae, breaking down dead coral in the process to form sand that eventually makes up the white coral sand beaches. Reefs are so crowded that many animals have had to develop ways to avoid being eaten or even sat on. One of the most effective methods is to become poisonous or develop dangerous spines, like the sea urchins. Reefs are often damaged by hurricanes and storms that break coral branches and topple whole colonies. But their greatest threat at present is from human activity. Ships and divers wreck fragile corals. Corals also die if sea temperature increases and there are fears that global warming might kill many coral reefs.

Coral jewels

The beautiful red and pink coral used to make jewelry does not come from coral reefs. It grows in deeper, cooler waters mainly in the Mediterranean where it is often found in caves and under overhangs, and also in the Pacific where large beds of it are found on seamounts.

Crown-of-thorns

The crown-of-thorns starfish *(left)* feeds on corals, sucking the living tissue up through its stomach and leaving the white coral skeletons. Outbreaks of these starfish have killed corals on many reefs, particularly in Australia.

A reef at night

A coral reef is quite different at night *(below)*. Many corals expand their tentacles and some fish go to sleep among the corals, like the parrotfish that wraps itself in a protective mucous blanket that it secretes each night *(bottom)*. The amazing flashlight fish is nocturnal and has a large gland under its eye that contains luminous bacteria that can be switched on and off.

EXPLORING THE OCEANS

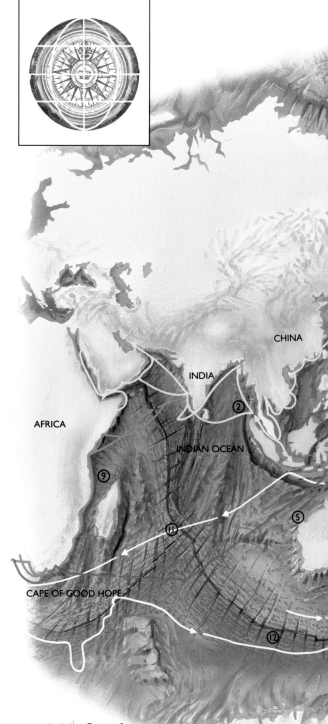

EARLY explorations of the oceans were largely driven by the need or desire to find new food and wealth, to achieve greater power, to spread religion — or out of simple curiosity. Another aim was to find better routes to places that were already known, although these voyages often resulted in the discovery of new lands. Many other peoples besides Europeans undertook such journeys. The Polynesians began colonizing the Pacific about 3,500 years ago. The Chinese explored the Asian seas in their junks and the Arabs, in their dhows, had charted much of the East African coast and reached India well before the Portuguese reached this area.

The Vikings

The Vikings explored the North Atlantic in the 9th and 10th centuries and reached North America. They set out from Scandinavia in their long ships, powered by about 60 rowers, to find new lands. Norse sagas say Iceland was so named because at that time it was so cold the fjords would freeze. In A.D. 982 the Viking Erik the Red found Greenland, at that time a much greener and more fertile land than Iceland.

VOYAGES OF EXPLORATION

①   **VIKINGS 9TH-10TH CENTURIES**
②   **ZHENG HE 1431-1433**

IN THE SERVICE OF SPAIN

③   **CHRISTOPHER COLUMBUS 1492-1493**
④   **AMERIGO VESPUCCI 1499-1500**
⑤   **MAGELLAN AND DEL CANO 1519-1522**
⑥   **ALVARO DE SAAVEDRA 1527-1528**

IN THE SERVICE OF FRANCE

⑦   **GIOVANNI DA VERRAZZANO 1524**

IN THE SERVICE OF PORTUGAL

⑧   **BARTOLOMEU DIAS 1487-1488**
⑨   **VASCO DA GAMA 1487-1498**
⑩   **AMERIGO VESPUCCI 1501-1502**

JAMES COOK

⑪   **FIRST VOYAGE 1768-1771**
⑫   **SECOND VOYAGE 1772-1775**
⑬   **THIRD VOYAGE (WITH CLERKE) 1776-1780**

The Portuguese

The Portuguese were the great ocean explorers of the 15th century. They explored much of the west African coast, in search of gold and with the additional aim of converting Muslims to Christianity. Bartolomeu Dias sailed the full length of Africa in 1488 and rounded the Cape of Good Hope. When the land route to China was blocked by the Turks, the main aim was to find a sea route to the east. In 1497-98 Vasco da Gama sailed from Portugal to India, and opened the important spice trade routes with Southeast Asia. It was also a Portuguese, Ferdinand Magellan, who led an expedition (in the service of Spain) that completed the first circumnavigation of the world, a voyage that lasted from 1519 to 1522. He was killed in the Philippines and the expedition returned under Sebastian del Cano.

CHINA

INDIA

AFRICA

INDIAN OCEAN

CAPE OF GOOD HOPE

Scrimshaw

Right up until the last century, voyages on sailing and whaling ships could last for months or years, and in fine weather sailors had plenty of time for hobbies. Scrimshaw, the carving and engraving of whale teeth and bones and walrus tusks, was one of the most popular in the 19th century and developed into an art, particularly on the whaling vessels from the northeastern United States. The pictures are usually of ships and whaling, biblical or romantic scenes. The engravings were blackened with ink or any available dark pigment.

GREENLAND

ICELAND

SCANDINAVIA

GREAT BRITAIN

①

⑦

ATLANTIC OCEAN

PORTUGAL

SPAIN

⑬

③

BAHAMAS

AFRICA

HAWAII

④

⑤

⑧

⑥

⑤

PAPUA N GUINEA

PACIFIC OCEAN

⑪

⑨

⑤

⑫

USTRALIA

⑫

⑪

⑪

⑫

⑫

NEW ZEALAND

⑩

⑫

STRAIT OF MAGELLAN

47

Columbus

In 1492 Christopher Columbus set sail from Spain, having failed to raise sponsorship from the Portuguese for his expedition.

In his flagship *Santa Maria*, with two other small ships and 120 men, he crossed the Atlantic hoping to find a quicker route to Asia and so give the Spaniards an advantage over the Portuguese who used the route around Africa. He landed in the Bahamas and continued on to Cuba, Haiti, and the Dominican Republic. On later journeys he discovered many other Caribbean islands as well as the coasts of Central and South America. After his death other explorers continued to explore the New World, including Amerigo Vespucci, for whom America is named.

Navigation

For ocean travel, navigation is a critical art. The Greeks developed a variety of instruments, including the astrolabe, which was used to map stars. The use of the magnetic compass became widespread in the 12th century. Used with charts, sailors could navigate out of sight of land. Latitude could be calculated by measuring the angle of the sun or stars above the horizon with a sextant. In 1735, the invention of the chronometer meant that accurate time could be kept on board ship, so that the distance from Greenwich, England, and thus the longitude, could be measured.

ASTROLABE

SEXTANT

COMPASS

CHRONOMETER

The early transoceanic voyages are among the most impressive because of the enormous difficulties and hardships that explorers and their crews had to face. Ships were cramped, uncomfortable, and unhygienic, and there was no way of keeping food fresh. Scurvy, a disease caused by lack of vitamin C, was a major problem. Vasco da Gama lost two-thirds of his crew on his voyage to India at the end of the 15th century. Scurvy could be prevented by eating fresh fruit, and Captain Cook lost no one on his second round-the-world journey in 1772, by insisting on an improved diet for his crew.

The Spirit of St. Louis

THE oceans were as much a challenge to early airplanes as they were to other methods of transport. The American Charles Lindbergh was the first person to fly alone nonstop across the Atlantic. A high-wing, single-engine monoplane was specially built for the

Kon-Tiki

To test the theory that the Polynesians originated in South America, crossing the Pacific in their canoes, Thor Heyerdahl tried the voyage in his balsa craft, Kon-Tiki. Although he successfully covered the 4,000 miles, anthropologists and historians have since proved that the Polynesians originated in Southeast Asia.

The voyages of Captain Cook

THE Englishman James Cook undertook three major voyages around the world between 1768 and 1779. He used the new navigational aids available in the 18th century to map the coasts of Papua New Guinea, New Zealand, and eastern Australia. He discovered many of the islands of the North and South Pacific, and crossed the Arctic and Antarctic circles. His final voyage was to find a northwest passage near Vancouver, but he failed. On his return, he stopped at Hawaii, which he had discovered on the outward journey. To the horror of his colleagues and crew, he was killed in a sudden quarrel with the local people.

Lone yachtsman
Joshua Slocum was the first person to sail single-handed around the world. He left Nova Scotia in his small wooden boat *Spray* in 1895 and returned to the same spot in 1898. He continued to sail alone until 1909, when he and his boat disappeared.

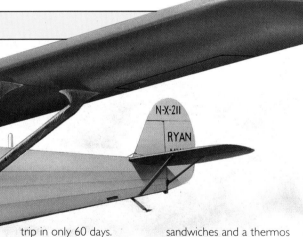

Another problem was that navigation instruments were extremely limited. Polynesian navigators could detect land by the color of the sea, clouds, presence of birds, or simply the smell. In Europe, methods of calculating latitude (distance from the North Pole) were available by the 1480s but longitude (distance east or west) remained a problem until the 18th century.

Since routes across the oceans have been established, travelers have had to find other ways of achieving the same sense of adventure, by recreating early voyages, such as the Kon-Tiki, or lone yachting.

trip in only 60 days. Lindbergh helped to assemble each part of it himself. It was named the *Spirit of St. Louis* for the city that had financed the project. He chose a single engine as he wanted to minimize the number of potential mechanical problems. To cut down on weight he took no radio or parachute — only sandwiches and a thermos of coffee! In 1927 he successfully made the crossing from New York to Paris, in 33 hours 30 minutes, winning a prize of $25,000. Today, transatlantic flights take about seven hours, with Concorde, flying at supersonic speed, making the crossing in only three hours.

Zheng He
The 15th-century Chinese admiral Zheng He was one of the earliest ocean explorers. In his junk, he led voyages from China west to the Red Sea and East Africa, and south to Indonesia. The ocean-going junks of his time were larger than any ships built in the West at that time.

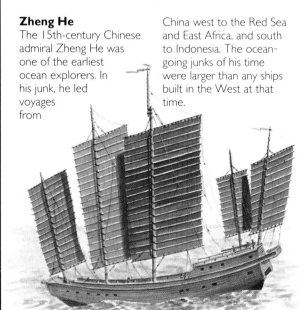

Egyptian papyrus boat

Some of the earliest ships were built in Egypt and were made of tapered reed bundles bound together like logs. This was because there were few trees in the region, only huge areas of swamp that provided papyrus. These boats were probably about 35 feet long.

Greek trireme

The classical Greek "galleys," usually used as warships, were up to 100 feet long and 20 feet wide. The power of the galley was increased by having oarsmen at several levels. A bireme had two banks or decks of oars, a trireme (left) had three.

Triremes had as many as 170 oarsmen, with an additional crew of about 30 including a flutist!

Early Mediterranean ships relied on oars, but in northern Europe many ships had sails. These could only be used if the wind blew in the right direction. Careful positioning of the sails later meant that ships could sail against the wind. This made possible the great voyages of discovery of the 15th and 16th centuries.

Large sailing ships reached their full development in the clipper ships of the mid-1800s. By this time, however, the first oceangoing steamers, powered by screw propellers, were plying the seas.

Cruise liners

It is only in this century that ocean travel has become comfortable enough for people to go to sea purely for fun. Early travelers would join cargo vessels to see the world. The first cruise liners were built in the early 1900s and soon developed into huge luxury floating hotels.

The largest was the *Norway*: originally called the *France*, it was launched in 1961.

Floating castles

GALLEONS were the main sailing ships from 1500 to 1700. Looking much like floating castles, most had four masts and were square-rigged. Spanish galleons plied the trade routes of the Atlantic and Pacific in the 17th and 18th centuries.

Hydrofoils

The hydrofoil is one of the fastest modern boats. Stilts supported by underwater wings lift the hydrofoil's hull out of the water when it travels at speed. This cuts down on the "drag" that slows up all vessels. Unfortunately, the hydrofoil's high fuel consumption makes it too expensive for long-distance travel, but it is used by ferry services throughout the world. The picture (right) shows a modern jet-propelled hydrofoil.

Computer ship

The *Shinaitoku Maru* was launched in 1980. Its two sets of rectangular sails are made of canvas stretched over steel frames. The ship also has a diesel engine. A computer monitors wind speed and direction and controls the sails, closing or opening them as required.

SHIPWRECKS

Truk Lagoon

Numerous wrecked ships lie scattered over the Pacific seabed as a legacy of the Second World War, but the most famous are those of Truk Lagoon in the Federated States of Micronesia. In 1944 U.S. bombers took by surprise a fleet of 60 Japanese merchant vessels and warships that had taken refuge in the lagoon. They sank every ship; over 1,000 men drowned. The fleet, scattered over the floor of the 40-mile-wide lagoon in about 250 feet of water, forms an enormous artificial reef and has become a popular diving site. Ships, such as the aircraft carrier *Fujikawa Maru (below)*, are now encrusted with coral, algae, sponges, and other invertebrate life. Huge numbers of fish, including sharks, take shelter in the holds and cabins. The

EVEN for the best-built ships, the sea is a dangerous place. Storms are the main causes of losses, but many shipwrecks are the result of war at sea, bad navigation, or simple human error. For archaeologists and historians shipwrecks are literally buried treasure. They provide "time capsules," showing how life was being lived at the time the ship went down. Preservation of wrecks has become a major science.

Even today there are still many accidents at sea, partly because the main shipping routes have become so crowded. For example, over 300,000 ships pass through the Straits of Dover each year.

wrecks have been designated a historical monument and no objects may be removed from them. Another famous casualty of the war was the German battleship *Bismarck*. It was sunk in the Atlantic in 1941 and now lies in more than 15,500 feet of water.

The *Titanic*

The *Titanic* was a British passenger liner, in her day the world's largest cruise ship. Many people thought her unsinkable. She was lost on her maiden voyage from Southampton to New York when she collided with a small iceberg just before midnight on April 14, 1912. The ship sank in just over two hours with the loss of about 1,500 lives. Seven hundred and eleven people were rescued. It

In 1982 a Turkish sponge diver discovered what proved to be the oldest-known shipwreck at Ulu Burun off the coast of Turkey. It dates from the 14th century B.C. and carried a huge range of valuable goods from all round the Mediterranean, including four-handled copper ingots.

TRUK ISLANDS

0   10mi

was not until a joint U.S.-French search project went to work in 1984-85, that the wreck was located.

EXPLOITING THE OCEANS

FOR centuries we have used the oceans as a source of food, minerals, and other valuable products, as a means of transport, and more recently for leisure activities. Seaweeds make good fertilizers, and are a source of substances used as thickeners in food. Salt has been extracted from seawater for over 4,000 years, and many minerals are mined offshore. The seabed is a source of sand and gravel for construction, and in some places huge quantities of dead shells are dredged and broken up to make cement.

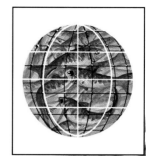

Pearls
Pearls are produced by pearl oysters *(below)*, when layers of nacre, or mother-of-pearl, are laid down around a speck of sediment or other foreign object inside the oyster's shell.

Krill

KRILL are the largest crustaceans in the rich plankton in the Southern Ocean. They feed on other plankton. "Superswarms" of krill can be several miles wide and weigh up to two million tons. They are eaten by fish, penguins, other seabirds, and baleen whales. A single whale can get through four to five tons of krill in 24 hours. Since 1976, humans have been taking about 500,000 tons of krill a year, using them for food or fish meal. However, it is important that we do not overexploit krill as this could endanger whales and other animals that feed on krill.

ANTARCTICA

■ MAIN AREAS OF KRILL DISTRIBUTION

Offshore oil
Oil and gas form from the tiny plants and animals that lived in the sea millions of years ago. After they died and sank to the sea floor, they were covered in layers of sand and mud. The combination of pressure and a sealed environment turned them into droplets of oil trapped in tiny holes in the rock like water in a sponge.

In some places oil lies a mile below the present seabed. Oil rigs *(right)* have a drill which bores into the rock; the oil or gas is then pumped up and taken to land by pipelines or tankers. Offshore oil provides about one quarter of the world's total, or about 15 million barrels a day.

Manganese nodules

Manganese nodules are strange lumps found on the seabed. They form when elements in seawater are deposited around fragments of material such as fish bones and shark teeth. They contain high concentrations of nickel, cobalt, and copper, all of which are useful to humans. The best nodules are found where there is little sediment and stable conditions, as in the large deep ocean basins. There are an estimated 1,500 trillion tons of nodules in the Pacific.

Tidal power

The sea generates energy through waves and tides that can be converted into a form we can use. The world's first commercially operated tidal power barrage is on the River Rance in Brittany, France (below). As the tide rises and passes through tunnels in the dam, water drives propellers of an engine in the tunnels, producing electricity.

Tourism

The sea and its shores are the most popular holiday destinations. Sandy beaches, cliffs, and scenic coastlines draw millions of visitors and there are many leisure activities to be enjoyed in or on the ocean, such as surfing, sailing, scuba diving, snorkeling (above), and fishing. Even the high seas are now used by the tourist industry, with big cruise ships sailing across the oceans to visit remote islands.

Fishing

Today, fish provide about 15 percent of all animal protein consumed. Fish products are used for animal feed, fertilizers, and soaps. Some modern fishing vessels have equipment that can take an entire shoal from the sea in one haul. Care has to be taken that catches do not exceed the rate at which a stock replenishes itself.

53

It is possible to increase the abundance of fish in some places. One method is to build artificial reefs. These act like coral reefs, providing shelter for fish and invertebrates. Once they become covered with seaweed, corals, and other animals they provide a perfect fish habitat. They are best if made of concrete or bamboo, but tires and even old cars are sometimes used.

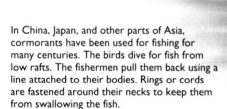

In China, Japan, and other parts of Asia, cormorants have been used for fishing for many centuries. The birds dive for fish from low rafts. The fishermen pull them back using a line attached to their bodies. Rings or cords are fastened around their necks to keep them from swallowing the fish.

Fishing the traditional way

EARLY humans used very simple methods for fishing, and these are still used in many countries. The simplest are harpoons and hooks-and-lines. Fishermen use small boats such as dug-out canoes and usually stay close to shore. The invention of nets meant that large numbers of fish could be caught at once. To find shoals, traditional fishermen watch seabirds and look for ripples on the surface of the sea. Fish can also be caught in traps, while mollusks, crabs, and small fish are collected by hand or by digging when walking over coral reefs, rocks, or muddy shores at

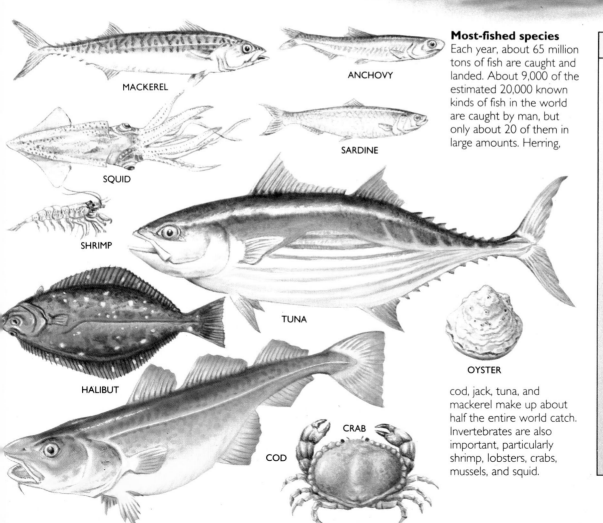

Most-fished species

Each year, about 65 million tons of fish are caught and landed. About 9,000 of the estimated 20,000 known kinds of fish in the world are caught by man, but only about 20 of them in large amounts. Herring, cod, jack, tuna, and mackerel make up about half the entire world catch. Invertebrates are also important, particularly shrimp, lobsters, crabs, mussels, and squid.

MACKEREL

ANCHOVY

SQUID

SARDINE

SHRIMP

HALIBUT

TUNA

OYSTER

COD

CRAB

Taking the catch

COMMERCIAL fishing fleets go to sea in large ships and may be away several months. They often have a factory ship that processes or refrigerates the fish. Sonar equipment and even space satellites may be used for locating schools of fish. Shoaling species such as anchovies are taken in purse seines. Tuna in the open seas are fished with drift nets stretched for

DRIFT OR GILL NET

low tide.

Some fishermen have very specialized methods. In Mauritania, fishermen throw out their nets when dolphins swim close to shore intending to round up shoals of fish on which to feed themselves. In Sri Lanka, some fishermen sit on tall stilts to have a good view of fish below, without the fish seeing them.

Fish preservation
Fish must be preserved if they are to be kept for any length of time. The simplest method is to dry them in the sun on racks. Other ways include smoking or soaking in very salty water called brine. The most common methods of preservation used today are refrigeration and canning.

Humans have gathered food from the sea since prehistoric times. In Japan and Iceland, fish is eaten in much greater quantities than meat, and some Pacific islanders rely almost entirely on fish for protein. Over one quarter of the world catch is converted into fish oil, animal feed, and fertilizers or used in products such as soaps and drugs. The world fishery catch is over 90 million tons a year, a big increase since the 1950s when only about 20 million tons were taken annually. In addition, about 24 million tons a year are taken by local fishermen and eaten in their own villages. The increase is because of the growing human population and the development of more efficient methods of catching fish. Unfortunately, it has led to overexploitation of the world's commercial fisheries.

World fishing grounds
The biggest commercial fisheries are in the northern Pacific and northern Atlantic. The world's top fishing nations are Japan, the U.S.S.R., and China. Countries now have the rights to fishing within 200 miles of their coasts. The richest fishing grounds are the continental shelves and areas of upwelling, where cold water rich in plankton and food rises to the surface. Vast quantities of anchovy used to be caught off Peru but the catch dropped dramatically after a succession of damaging El Niños (see page 9).

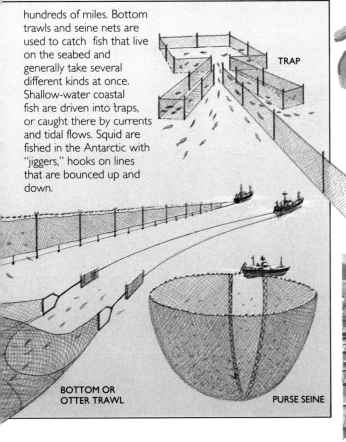

hundreds of miles. Bottom trawls and seine nets are used to catch fish that live on the seabed and generally take several different kinds at once. Shallow-water coastal fish are driven into traps, or caught there by currents and tidal flows. Squid are fished in the Antarctic with "jiggers," hooks on lines that are bounced up and down.

TRAP

BOTTOM OR OTTER TRAWL

PURSE SEINE

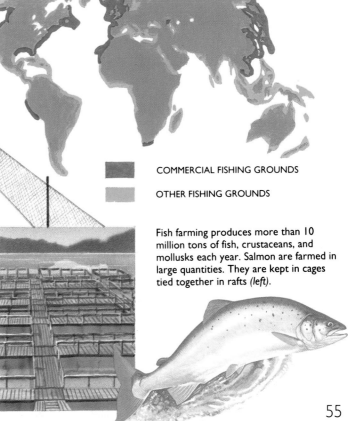

COMMERCIAL FISHING GROUNDS

OTHER FISHING GROUNDS

Fish farming produces more than 10 million tons of fish, crustaceans, and mollusks each year. Salmon are farmed in large quantities. They are kept in cages tied together in rafts (left).

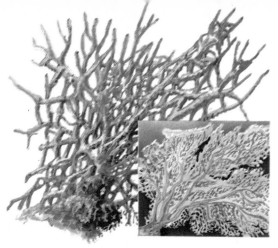

Killing coral

Coral reefs are damaged by tourists and ships. Corals also "bleach" (turn white) and may die if stressed by increased sea temperatures or some pollutants. They are also easily suffocated by silt, washed off the coast or down rivers as a result of deforestation, or stirred up from the sea bottom during dredging.

Polluting the oceans

SOME pollution in the oceans comes from ships or offshore operations, but a large proportion results from human activities on land. Oil, sewage, and garbage are some of the pollutants we dispose of in the sea.

Over three million tons of oil are discharged into the oceans each year, about half from ships and half from on-shore operations.

Plankton blooms, or red tides, are sudden vast population explosions of plankton caused by increased nutrients in the water, usually from sewage or agricultural runoff containing fertilizers. Large quantities of waste uses up oxygen in the water in the process of rotting. Eventually, even the seabed can be starved of oxygen, as in the Baltic Sea where nearly half of the deep waters are now virtually devoid of life.

Garbage in the oceans has increased dramatically since the invention of plastics and other synthetic materials that are buoyant and do not disintegrate (some can survive for as long as 50 years). Plastic containers, packaging, and a wide variety of toys float to remote areas on the ocean currents. Turtles and whales die from eating floating plastic that looks like jellyfish.

POLLUTION

SEVERE

PERSISTENT

MEDITERRANEAN SEA

Mediterranean pollution

The Mediterranean is bordered by 18 countries, with at least 120 major major cities that pour sewage and industrial wastes into the sea. As it is almost landlocked, pollutants are not washed away as in the open sea, and they tend to become more concentrated over time. Hundreds of striped dolphins died in the Mediterranean in 1990. A virus was found in some of them similar to one found in seals that died in the North Sea over the same period. These diseases may be linked to pollution, although this has not yet been confirmed.

In 1975, Mediterranean countries jointly set up an Action Plan to fight pollution. There has been no increase in pollution since then, but there are still many problems to be solved.

OIL SPILL

PLANKTON BLOOM

Oiled seabirds

SEABIRDS are very vulnerable to oil spills as oil destroys the waterproofing of their feathers and they become waterlogged. While trying to clean themselves, they eat the oil which then poisons them. Up to 30,000 birds are thought to have died as a result of oil spills during the 1991 Gulf War. The *Exxon Valdez*, a supertanker that went aground in 1989 in Prince William Sound, Alaska, spilled 11 million gallons of oil, killing over 36,000 seabirds and 1,000 sea otters, and affecting over 1,000 miles of coastline.

ABOUT 150,000 tons of plastic nets and lines are discarded by fishermen each year, over 500 miles of plastic fishing nets in the North Pacific alone. These entangle turtles, seabirds, and many marine mammals. Today, much fishing is carried out with fine plastic drift nets that are so large and sheer they cannot be seen by diving birds or detected by dolphins with their sonar. Commercial fishing fleets may set up to 20,000 miles of net a day in the fishing season with a single net stretching for up to 30 miles. They are used in all oceans for catching tuna, squid, salmon, and other fish. In the Pacific about 100,000 dolphins and millions of birds have been killed by becoming entangled in these nets. Other modern fishing methods also kill animals accidentally in large numbers; for example, shrimp trawls that catch turtles.

Since about three quarters of the world's population lives on the coast, it is not surprising that the oceans are suffering from pollution and other human activities. Unfortunately, people have always thought of the oceans as rubbish dumps. Even people living inland are not blameless; rivers carry 9.3 billion tons of silt and waste to coastal waters each year. Coastal habitats, such as marshes, are threatened by the building of ports, factories, tourist resorts, and other developments and these are the areas where marine plant and animal life is richest.

GARBAGE

Dinoflagellates are the tiny plankton that suddenly bloom and cause red tides when the level of nutrients rises in seawater. Species called *Gonyaulax* and *Glymnodium* can be highly poisonous and can contaminate seafood that we eat.

Dynamite fishing
In some countries, fishermen use methods that cause serious damage to the seabed. In the Philippines, dynamite explosions stun the fish that then float to the surface where they can be collected in a net. But these explosions also kill the coral reef and many other plants and animals.

Mangrove destruction
Mangroves are being cut down worldwide for timber, fuelwood and wood chips. In the Philippines, the total area of mangroves declined from 13,000 square miles to only 1,000 square miles between 1920 and 1988. In many countries, such as Ecuador and Indonesia, mangroves are destroyed to make ponds for rearing prawns and fish.

The main forms of pollution are sewage and industrial waste. Chemicals, pesticides, and other industrial products are common pollutants and have been found in penguins, arctic seals, and even in rat-tail fish at a depth of 10,000 feet. Beluga whales in the St Lawrence River in North America, whose population has dropped from 5,000 to 100, have themselves become toxic; they contain the highest levels of poisons found in any marine mammal.

In some countries, particularly in the Pacific, coastal villagers traditionally "own" nearby areas of sea and coral reef and have the right to fish there. They are usually careful not to take too many fish and not to use damaging fishing methods. Sometimes they stop fishing for part of the year or in a particular place to allow fish stocks to recover.

Conserving the reefs

All round the world efforts are being made to prevent further damage to coral reefs. In Indonesia, a large marine park is being set up to protect the reefs and threatened animals (1). The marine parks at Eilat, in the Red Sea (2), and Buck Island, in the U.S. Virgin Islands (3), have underwater nature trails for divers. Mooring buoys on reefs in Hawaii (4), American Samoa (5), Florida (6), and other places in the Caribbean stop boats from anchoring on fragile corals.

Some overexploited reef animals are "farmed" or raised in tanks, such as the queen conch in the Turks and Caicos islands in the Caribbean (7), giant clams in the Solomon Islands (8), and trochus snails, that provide the valuable mother-of-pearl shell, in Palau in the Pacific (9).

At 133,000 square miles the Great Barrier Reef Marine Park off Australia is the largest coral reef reserve in the world (*right* and 10 on map). It is divided into zones for research scientists, tourists, and fishermen.

New mangrove forests

Attempts are now being made to restore mangrove forests that have been very badly damaged. In several countries, such as India, Bangladesh, and Ecuador, small seedlings are planted out in the mud in areas where the forests have been destroyed.

REEFS

CAIRNS

CORAL SEA

TOWNSVILLE

0   100m

CORAL REEFS

LOGGERHEAD TURTLE

BLUE WHALE

SEA OTTER

These traditional forms of conservation have broken down in many areas, but people are now realizing how important it is to maintain them wherever possible.

Pollution, and overfishing in the open oceans outside countries' exclusive fishing zones, are more difficult problems to deal with. Often nations have to work together to find solutions. Many countries have drawn up treaties and

Protected species?

Most threatened marine species are now legally protected, although unfortunately this does not always mean that they are not killed. Many seals and whales are protected, but there is still much concern over the future of some whales as countries such as Norway, Japan, and the U.S.S.R. still wish to continue whaling.

The best hope for the future of the giant clam lies in the farming projects being started in many countries. Sea otter populations have recovered dramatically since this species has been protected. Turtles are protected in most countries and trade in their shells, skins, and meat is banned.

Whale-watching

THE tourist industry can play an important role in protecting the marine environment, on which it depends in so many countries. Whale-watching trips *(below)* are a way of making an income from whales without killing them. Hotels, scuba diving businesses, and other tourist operators are now helping to protect coral reefs. Some hotels set up reserves to educate tourists about the fragility of coral reefs. Clean beaches are essential to the tourist industry, and in Europe official standards have now been set to limit sewage pollution.

MONK SEAL

GIANT CLAM

Saving the turtles

Many turtle populations are declining because the eggs are eaten by humans or other predators, or nesting females are disturbed by tourists. In Pakistan, and many other countries, nesting beaches are now patrolled at night. Guards remove eggs to artificial nests in protected enclosures. When the baby turtles hatch, they are released into the sea. These projects help local people to understand why turtle eggs should not be taken and can also provide a tourist attraction.

regional conventions with each other in which they agree to work together to stop pollution and overfishing.

Marine parks and reserves have been set up in numerous countries to protect threatened marine species and vulnerable habitats such as mangroves, coral reefs, swamps, and estuaries.

We can all play a part in helping to protect the oceans. We can visit marine parks and reserves, learn about marine life, and support conservation organizations that are working to save the seas. We can recycle plastic, glass, and paper to cut down on waste, and avoid buying products that use a lot of energy. When visiting the coast and sea, we can make sure that we do not pollute it or damage its precious marine life.

Rainbow Warrior

MANY conservation organizations have helped save threatened marine animals and their ocean habitats. The World Wildlife Fund (WWF) has helped to set up marine parks in many countries and has supported projects to protect turtles, whales, and seals. The International Marinelife Alliance works in the Philippines (11 on map), training Philippine fishermen to catch aquarium fish with nets instead of using poison, which damages coral reefs.

Greenpeace has paid particular attention to the survival of the oceans. Its best known ship, *Rainbow Warrior*, was named after a legendary Red Indian tribe called the "Warriors of the Rainbow" who, it was said, would restore the Earth to its former beauty. Greenpeace has mounted campaigns against testing nuclear weapons in the Pacific, against whaling and sealing, and against the dumping of chemical and radioactive wastes in the oceans. Greenpeace members often take dramatic action to achieve their aims, for example, placing themselves in the paths of large whaling boats. They have also persuaded people to stop buying brands of canned tuna that have been taken with drift nets, which kill dolphins.

GLOSSARY

Abyssal plain Extensive flat area of the ocean floor formed by sediment, washed off the continents, lying over the ocean crust.

Asthenosphere The hot, molten inner layer of the Earth.

Astrolabe An instrument used to map the stars.

Atoll A coral island made up of a reef surrounding a lagoon.

Baleen Horny plates that hang from the jaws of toothless whales and are used for straining plankton from the water.

Beaufort scale A system used to describe the strength of the wind at sea, using signs that can be seen by the naked eye.

Benthic Animals and plants that live on or in the ocean floor.

Blubber A thick layer of insulating fat under the skin of cetaceans and seals.

Breach The way in which whales and dolphins leap out of the water.

Cetacean The group of animals comprising whales, dolphins, and porpoises.

Clipper A large, fast sailing ship that carried cargo across the major oceans in the last century.

Continental rise The rise often found at the base of the continental slope formed by the sediment that rolls down.

Continental shelf The part of a continent that extends out below the surface of the sea.

Continental slope The steep slope that drops off from the edge of the continental shelf to the ocean floor.

Convergence Place in the ocean where currents meet, usually causing water to sink.

Coral reef A stony structure formed from living corals and numerous other invertebrates, plants, and fish, found in tropical seas.

Crustaceans Invertebrate group characterized by hard outer skeletons and jointed legs.

Cyclone Violent storm (also called hurricane or typhoon) that occurs when warm, moist air rises over tropical oceans.

Delta The muddy or sandy mouth of a large river, broken into numerous channels, and formed by sediment brought down by the river.

Denticles Tiny tooth-like projections that cover the skin of sharks and some other animals.

Divergence Place in the sea where currents part, usually causing water to rise.

Gill Feather-like organ found in many marine invertebrates and fish that is used for respiration.

Hot spot Place where hot magma rises to the surface of the ocean bed and forms chains of volcanoes, as the plates move over it.

Invertebrate Large group of animals, including insects, mollusks, and crustaceans, that have no backbone or internal skeleton.

Latitude Distance north and south of the equator.

Lithosphere The rigid outer surface of the Earth.

Longitude Distance east or west of Greenwich, England.

Mangrove Tree that grows on muddy coasts in tropical countries whose roots are adapted to regular flooding by high tides, salty water, and lack of oxygen.

Migration	The movement of an animal from one part of the world to another on a regular basis (for example, annually or seasonally to find food or breeding areas).
Mollusks	A large group of invertebrates that includes snails, slugs, bivalves, octopuses, squids, and many others, many of which have protective shells.
Monsoon	A season characterized by different patterns of winds and rainfall that occurs in some parts of the tropics.
Navigation	The skill of getting vehicles or vessels from one place to another.
Neap tide	Tide that occurs when the sun and moon are at right angles to the Earth, giving the smallest tidal range.
Ocean ridge	A long range that rises above the seafloor as a result of new seafloor welling up from inside the Earth.
Ocean trench	A long, narrow, very deep valley found near the edge of continents or island chains, also called subduction zone as this is where one plate moves under another.
Pack ice	The layer of ice floating on the sea, formed when the sea freezes, which constantly breaks up and becomes "packed" together again.
Pelagic	Living or growing at or near the surface of the ocean, as certain animals or plants.
Plankton	The tiny plants (phytoplankton) and animals (zooplankton) that float in the surface layers of the oceans and provide food for numerous marine animals.
Scrimshaw	Whale teeth, bones, and walrus tusks carved or engraved with pictures.
Sextant	Instrument used to measure the angle of the sun and stars above the horizon.
Sonar	A device used for locating and measuring the distance of other objects underwater.
Spring tide	Tide that occurs when the sun and moon are in line with the Earth, giving the largest tidal range.
Stromatolites	Hard, cushion-like structures, formed by blue-greens, that are the earliest forms of life in the sea.
Submersible	An underwater vessel, much smaller and more maneuverable than a submarine that usually has some kind of motor and can carry passengers.
Swim bladder	The air sac found in bony fish that prevents them from sinking.
Thermal vent	A "chimney" found in some parts of the deepest oceans where sulphur-rich hot water from below the Earth's crust is released.
Thermocline	An abrupt temperature change in tropical oceans at about 1,000 feet where deep cold waters meet warm surface waters.
Tidal range	The difference in height between high and low tides.
Turbidity current	An underwater avalanche that flows down the continental slope, carrying huge quantities of sediment.
Upwelling	Cold waters that rise up from the deep into warmer surface waters, often found at divergences.
Water spout	A whirling mass of air that forms over warm water when rising, warm, moist air meets cold, dry air.
Whirlpool	A circular movement of water caused when two currents meet or when strong tides and currents meet.

INDEX

Dep. Legal B. 31.897-91

SUMMER COTTAGES
AND
CASTLES

SUMMER
COTTAGES AND CASTLES
Scenes from the Good Life

Patricia Corbin

Photographs by Ted Hardin

with additional photography by
Michael Skott, Kim Sargent, and Edward Oleksak

E. P. DUTTON, INC.   NEW YORK

First published, 1983,
in the United States by E.P. Dutton, Inc.,
2 Park Avenue, New York, N.Y. 10016

Library of Congress Catalog Card Number: 82-74248
ISBN: 0-525-93279-8

Published simultaneously in Canada by
Clarke, Irwin & Company, Limited, Toronto and Vancouver

Printed and bound by Dai Nippon Printing Co., Ltd.,
Tokyo, Japan.

10 9 8 7 6 5 4 3 2 1

First Edition

The flowers illustrated on the endpapers of this book were
photographed in the gardens of Island House, the summer home of
Mrs. Henry Parish II.

(Pages ii-iii) Old and new wicker lacquered a bright melon shade
and masses of red geraniums make a fresh color combination for a
sun-room perched at the edge of the sea.

(Frontispiece, page iv) The photograph by Ted Hardin is repro-
duced by kind permission of House Beautiful magazine, Hearst
Corporation.

Summer Scenes:

Having a Wonderful Summer

Summer is out-of-doors, to sail, swim, fish, search for shells and stones, to play strenuous tennis or leisurely golf, to have a flower or vegetable garden, to do all the things the season proclaims as *now*. Having a wonderful summer is a collage of the good life.

Having a wonderful summer is—
    someplace to go
and entertain in a greenhouse, feast in a forest,
    relax in a slat house, or have tea on the terrace,
to paint the dock
    or sail away,
    hang bathing suits out to dry,
    exercise the runabout,
    or just hang in a hammock and read or dream—

Someplace to go

Adirondacks carved bears enliven a
whimsical hat-and-umbrella stand
in the rustic style that was so
popular in the late 1800s.
Photograph by Michael Skott.

And entertain in a greenhouse

A swath of bright color surrounds a greenhouse, where all summer long, the more flowers that are picked, the more blooms there are. Opening onto a terrace and swimming pool, the room is an ideal party space for two or twenty.

Feast in a forest

with lunch under the trees, and green leaves forming a shady bower for a cool retreat. The paper lantern makes a low-hanging moon; cutoff tree trunks are handy side tables.

Relax in a slat house

An ethereal slat house designed by Peter Hoppner makes a wonderful outdoor room, with its lofty ceiling sheathed in Plexiglas. Primarily used for shading a large collection of ferns and begonias, the vaulted space does double duty for luncheons and dinners.

Have tea on the terrace

Drinking in the long view that meanders down through majestic trees to the water's rocky edge is the special delight of any meal enjoyed on this terrace.

$\mathcal{P}$aint the dock

A wonderful bit of summer fantasy this—a private dock doing its best to resemble a big-city bridge. Photograph by Michael Skott.

Or sail away

A navy training vessel sailing by the Jamestown, Rhode Island, shore.

Hang bathing suits out to dry

A long-dead pear tree makes a perfect drying post for the family's bathing suits and sun hats. Photograph by Michael Skott.

Exercise the runabout

The Boardman girls call their Model T the "summer convenience" and keep it chugging around running quick errands.

Or just hang in a hammock and read or dream—

Artist Veva Crozer enjoys a rare rest period in her favorite summer spot. Photograph by Michael Skott.

CONTENTS

Castellated Waterlot was built of shingle and stone in the late 1890s by an artist without benefit of an architect. The inside is board-and-batten construction, with arched stone fireplaces repeating the shape of the windows.

INTRODUCTION

Ever since the last hurricane (which sent waves of seawater crashing through the living room) our house has been unofficially known as Mildew Manor. Waterlot, the real name of the place, is a shingle and stone structure that wanders over the rocks in the most original and genial fashion—everything is on a different level—we walk up the stairs to the dining room, down to the living room, over and around to go into the bedrooms. It is quite easy to get a bit lost in our house, and guests often end up somewhere in the hall, searching vainly for the breakfast room. It can be an adven-

ture, which makes their visit much more exciting and Waterlot that much more interesting, or so we hope.

Summers are for having fun, and our eccentric house is made for fun—we treat it more like a playhouse than the real thing, although it needs constant repairs like any other real house near the ocean. For some reason our neighbors here at Price's Neck all have places that look more grown-up than ours. Maybe it is because their houses are seriously decorated and furnished with pieces that go together, not matching "suites," of course, but the sort of thing that is seemly and appropriate. Our

1

house is far from serious, certainly not decorated, and nothing goes together. To be absolutely honest, it is a look usually found only in thrift shops, attics, and basements. To explain what I mean, a brief description is necessary: the living room has yellow walls, an orange ceiling, grass-green curtains, a crystal chandelier, and pink and purple and coral and blue and Federal and Chippendale and Tudor and baroque and rococo, plus wicker, of course. We also have lots of FFF (fake French furniture) and heavy doses of Grand Rapids (especially in the bedrooms). There are some lively displays on tabletops: a stuffed toad standing up on his hind legs holding a tiny tambourine; an especially curious Penelope construction of string, kidney beans, and macaroni; and a basket of mussel shells spouting tall spires of pheasant feathers (every fall our neighbor, Jimmy Van Alen, has a shoot, and the walking wounded trail over to our property and drop their feathers). In an effort to upgrade I did have the ping-pong table moved out of the living room, which calmed things down some.

Needless to say Waterlot does not have the right stuff for *House Beautiful* (or for this book), but because we are crazy about it and love our summer life just the way it is, I got the idea of recording other people's summer places, the ones that I especially admire. They belong to old friends who love their houses just as much as we do ours; and although the decorating is different in each, the houses are alike in having one theme: great style. Some of the houses are just cottages, and some are more like castles, just as some are grand and others are very simple. Whatever the size or design, they all show the very personal pleasures and talents for summer living.

Newport, 1981

PLACES
AND
PLEASURES

The Porters' Spruce Head Island house, built from a prefab kit in the 1930s; the painting is by Aline Porter.

$\mathscr{P}$LACES
AND
$\mathscr{P}$LEASURES

Back in the days when kerosene lamps were vacation house necessities, summer places typically had split-bamboo shades that were lowered to screen the porch, some hammocks and rocking chairs for lazing around, iron beds and enameled washbasins in the bedrooms—nothing stylish, just useful equipment along with the other necessities of summer living: the water pump, the icebox, and the outhouse.

Nowadays, it is island life that is nearest to what a real summer place used to mean: a vacation from all mechanical conveniences—so basic and simple—without telephone or television, no neighbors and no noise. A summer house on one's own private island is just that, away from the world, a place to retreat and refuel for the complexities of modern life.

Eliot Porter, the renowned naturalist photographer, and his wife, Aline, who is an artist, live in such a place off the coast of Maine. It is their refuge for the summer months, built from a prefab kit some fifty-odd years ago and decorated in the most straightforward way: white paint for walls, floors sprinkled with homemade rag rugs, sheer white curtains at windows, beds covered with faded patchwork quilts. Mrs. Porter's inspiration for simplicity was R. Buckminster Fuller's house on Bear Island, also off the coast of Maine, whose pared-down crisp New England look she admired and copied.

In Narragansett Bay there is a prominent rock known as The Dumplings, an island much dreaded by seafarers who sailed into Newport harbor in the nineteenth century. Many ships, lost in the fog, struck the rock and sank. One beautiful barkentine did retain at least the ribs of her hull for many years after being dashed there in a storm. She was *The Gem*, famous for making scores of voyages to Africa, plying the slave and rum trade. In those days there was a fort with a rounded tower on the island; perched there now, spreading upward, is a shingled house called Clingstone. It was built in 1904 by a determined gentleman from Philadelphia who wanted a peaceful, isolated summer place. The house is shingled inside as well as out, has big windows, cavernous stone fireplaces, and winding stairs spiraling high. The source of power is a wind generator; bottled gas is used for the stove, saltwater for washing. Each summer the family (relatives of the original owner) arrives by boat. Like gypsies they land with a complete caravan of living equipment.

Another famous landmark off Newport is Gooseberry Island. From the late 1880s, and for over fifty years, the island was the meeting place for probably the world's most exclusive club—the Gooseberry Island Fishing Club, although no records show that anyone ever

The view from the Porters' house sweeps over rocks enveloped in a canopy of green sprinkled with tiny wildflowers. A gull's nest is in the foreground, and cropping up in the near distance is Barred Island; Isle au Haut stretches beyond in a mass of veiled blue. Photograph by Eliot Porter.

bothered to fish. (No women were ever allowed on the island, which added immensely to its exclusivity.) Membership was inherited and limited to only fifteen gentlemen. They paid $1,500 in dues for the privilege of swimming in the nude, drinking champagne, and lunching on clam chowder, steamed clams, lobster, and corn, topped off with a dessert of hot waffles and maple syrup.

The luncheons at Gooseberry Island are plain picnics now, and although it is still exclusive, the present owner often invites ladies to swim and to share his solitary splendor.

Poised at the edge of Hammersmith Farm, The Windmill, without the wind-generating sails and wheels of the real thing, stands as a landmark for fishermen and yachtsmen in Narragansett Bay. The house has proven to be such a navigational aid that the Rhode Island Coast Guard is considering putting a beacon light on top of it.

The original windmill, an old 1870s structure, used to sit in the middle of the cow barns at Hammersmith. The Auchinclosses had planned to move it down near the water and renovate, but, tragically, in 1966 The Windmill burned to the ground. The foundations were already built, so the family decided to go ahead and reconstruct the place as near in looks as possible to the old one; the children were invited to submit their own ideas and sketches for a new building. Jacqueline Kennedy Onassis won the competition, and the architect Anne Tillinghast turned her drawing into reality.

Octagon-shaped, with a fourth-floor gallery that circles a deck and studio room, the house is living in miniature, having a complete self-contained apartment twenty-two-feet wide on the main floor, with each succeeding level of the house being four feet smaller.

There are lots of castlelike summer houses that loom hugely up and down the eastern seaboard, but America is certainly not castle country in the true sense of crenellated and bastionlike strongholds. There are a few public ones that look like defensive fortifications: the seventeenth-century Florida fortress, Castillo de San Marcos; Ophir, in Purchase, New York, could be in the Scottish Highlands; Gillette's Castle is a medieval Rhenish-style one in Hadlyme, Connecticut; Abbadia Mare, inventor John Hays Hammond's, is in Gloucester, Massachusetts. Not far from Hammond's twelfth-century replica there is a curious summer house that is known as the cottage-that-grew-into-a-castle, and it is perhaps the most fascinating summer place in America, and surely the most deceiving from the outside—somber and medievallike describe the house that shambles over the cliffs at Gloucester. The stonework is menacingly gray; shingled turrets and towers loom high and brooding over the moss; the leaded windows are lancet-shaped and rather sinister. The house is genially named Beauport, however, and in spite of all the outside gloom it is just that, a pretty place full of wit and wonderful furnishings.

The designer of this extraordinary structure was Henry Davis Sleeper, a soft-spoken, gentle little man who became one of America's foremost interior decorators. He was a consultant to Henry Francis du Pont on the development of du Pont's great Winterthur Museum. Later he ranged far, moving from the staid eastern shore to the wilder coast of Hollywood, where his theatrical ways with light, color, and form were fully appreciated. Sleeper began his summer home at Eastern Point in 1907. It first consisted of three rooms moved from a little gambrel-roofed 1728 house in Essex, Massachusetts. From then on, parts and pieces of beams, doors, floors, mantels, moldings—all manner of architectural finework—were lugged, tugged, and put into place at Beauport. The resulting ingenious spaces showing off Sleeper's marvelous collections seem to flow from room to room with magical grace. It all works, to the eye's delight, and to this day it exists in forty-four rooms—a cottage-into-a-castle.

There is a privately owned castle in America that is now, surprisingly enough, a cheerful and attractive summer place for a young family. It is a remarkable for-tresslike design—the original owner, Sherman Fairchild, sent his two architects to Paris in the 1920s to find drawings and plans of medieval castles to copy. Begun in 1929 and finished three years later, the castle looks rather like a brick facsimile of the secluded Château Meung-sur-Loire, a twelfth-century fortification near Orleans with an illustrious history: it was used for six centuries as a *château de plaisance* for the bishops of Orleans, and in 1429 Joan of Arc lodged there during her campaign against the English. During World War II the castle was a bastion for the German high command.

Eastfair is a fairy-tale creation with a fairy-tale ending—ten years ago it was destined to be destroyed by a developer who wanted to carve up the property into two-acre parcels. Fortunately, the new owners came along and bought the place intact with the medieval and Gothic furnishings, along with thirty acres of land.

It is not a large castle, as castles go, but then only three people live there and to them the space is quite adequate, especially as it is primarily used as a summer home. The castle overlooks Long Island Sound; and the property includes a swimming pool, a proper moat, a boxwood parterre garden, some topiary, statuary, a maze, a duck pond, a vineyard (the family makes its

Clingstone, built in 1904, resembles the H. H. Richardson design for Stoughton House of 1882. The Newport bridge is in the background, and sailing majestically by is the Danish Lindø, *a former cargo ship, built in 1926 of mahogany and converted now to a sailing schooner. Her red sails are reminiscent of* The Gem's, *a cargo ship that met its fate on The Dumplings' rocks in the late nineteenth century.*

Gooseberry Island house was built in 1945 with the island's stones and has since withstood two hurricanes. For over fifty years the island was the meeting place of an exclusive gentlemen's club; the original clubhouse was demolished in the 1938 hurricane.

own estate wine), and a movie studio underground where the "oubliette" (secret dungeon) would have been. The massive stone dogs on sentinel duty in front of the castle were crafted in Italy. Another pair just like them was apparently the first set of dogs ordered by Mr. Fairchild, but for some reason it was considered flawed —the imperfect pair, now painted black with silver collars, has come to rest in front of a building on East 45th Street in New York City.

Castles create history, but cottages are homey; they are everyone's dream of a little low-maintenance place, the kind of housekeeping where you walk in the door, sweep out the cobwebs, empty the mousetraps, throw open the windows, and sure enough, with balmy days and hot summer sun, all is well. Real cottages (not the Newport kind) are our American dream houses. We visualize them as cozy and cute, their flower boxes spilling over with summer's blooms, their porches filled with wicker—a nostalgic picture, but a wonderfully true one that actually exists today in Oak Bluffs, Massachusetts (on Martha's Vineyard). The town's cluster of gingerbread cottages goes back more than 120 years, and they are glorious confections of the carpenter's art with names like Bell Buoy and Small Frey (both the Bell and the Frey families are longtime summer residents).

Oak Bluffs is a family place that began as a religious camp-meeting ground in 1835—tents were pitched and people came for a vacation combined with religious services—and by 1855 there were over 200 tents, so the resort business on Martha's Vineyard was well launched. A few years later the first jigsaw filigree cottage was shipped from Rhode Island to Wesleyan Grove to replace a family's tent, and from then on the transition to fancy cottages continued steadily. All the wonderful embellishments of gables and spires, Gothic doors and windows, give the little houses their ecclesiastical accents; and once a season, during the height of the summer, there is an Illumination, a festival of candlelight and Oriental lanterns that turns the cottages into a twinkling fairyland.

Oak Bluffs remains as it was back in the early days, with quiet summers of prayer meetings and hymn singings, choir concerts and Sunday services held in the Tabernacle in Trinity Park. The spirit of the community stays serene, having a sanctity that is refreshing, and because of the old-fashioned ways and charms, visitors often ask, "Do real people really live here?"

Most summer scenes are drastically different nowadays—the parties, pleasures, and pursuits have undergone major surgery since the turn of the century. But a hundred years ago society's entertainments were for the most part overly extravagant, elaborate, and long, with huge numbers of guests partaking of filling and rib-sticking food. The following menu, reprinted from *The New York Times*, is for a party in August:

Card of Refreshments

Fresh Salmon à la Montpellier	Galantine of Turkey
Woodcocks	Galantine of Ham
Chicken Partridges	Galantine of Tongue
Pickled Oysters	Boned Partridges in Jelly
Crisp Potatoes à la Downing	Croquettes of Chicken
Maraschino Jelly	Chicken Salad
Rum Jelly	Lobster Salad
Wine Jelly	Italian Salad
	Celery Salad
Golden Plover	Pâté de Foie Gras
Snipes	Pâté de Truffles
Fried Oysters	Scalloped Oysters
Soft Crabs	
Ice Creams: Vanilla, Almond,	Statuettes of Lafayette and
Pistachio, Strawberry, Lemon	Washington
Mille Fruits Ice	Vases of Fancy Creams
Mille Fruits Crème	Nesselrode Pudding
Variety of Sherbets	Plum Pudding Glacé
Fancy Ices	Meringue Baskets à la Crème
	Jelly Russe
Fancy Cakes	Charlotte Russe
	Bonbons

Peaches, apricots, pears, nectarines, and 250 pounds of black Hamburg grapes from Mr. Wetmore's own hothouse; 24 baskets of champagne frappe, and Amontillado sherry, 6 bowls of lemonade, Sangureis, Madeira, cognac, etc.

This splendid and ample assortment of garden-party food fed over 3,000 guests (some said it seemed like 10,000) in Newport one hot summer's day. The *fête champêtre* event was called "probably the greatest affair of its kind ever given in this country" by one of the enthusiastic guests. The very genial host of this great affair was William Shepard Wetmore, and the scene was his Château-sur-Mer, where dancing (and certainly eating) went on from ten in the morning to ten at night. As an extravagant and elegant example of a garden party, probably the Wetmore fête was the greatest affair, and

The Windmill at Hammersmith Farm is an octagon-shaped summer house that stands as a landmark for fishermen and yachtsmen in Narragansett Bay.

Apple green and crisp white bring the dining room at Beauport into sharp focus—the light, the colors, and the breathtaking view make the Golden Step Room (named after a ship model) a vivid background for marine memorabilia, green-patterned Fitzhugh export china, and a collection of green majolica. Photograph by David Bohl courtesy Society for the Preservation of New England Antiquities.

14

by all accounts, the longest ongoing one known to society. Elizabeth Drexel Lehr recounts another spectacular entertainment of the era:

We were standing in the garden at Beaulieu, the Cornelius Vanderbilt, Jr., home, and the scene around us was one of almost fairy-tale beauty, for it was the night of Grace Vanderbilt's great "Fête des Roses." A big harvest moon hung low in the inky velvet of the August sky; the lawns were lighted by myriads of shaded lamps, while fireworks played their glittering cascades of gold and silver. Red roses were everywhere, massed in gigantic baskets, hanging in festoons. Their fragrance perfumed the ballroom; they lay crushed under the feet of the guests on the velvet-carpeted avenue which led to the house. Gaily striped tents lined both sides of the avenue—tents of fortune tellers, booths containing a dozen different shows, coconut shies, miniature rifle ranges and all the rest. But the prizes, instead of being the ordinary showmen's trumpery, were all beautiful presents, gold and enamel vanity boxes for the women, cigarette cases for the men. In one part of the grounds a miniature theatre had been constructed. A hundred builders and carpenters had worked day and night for a week to have it ready for that one evening, fitted it out with a full-size stage and perfect lighting. The entire company of *Red Rose Inn* which was then having an enormous success in New York had been engaged and transported with scenery and baggage to Beaulieu to present the play to the guests. An expensive proceeding, this, for it had involved closing the theatre in New York for two nights.

Even picnics were elaborate affairs in those days and the more bucolic the setting, the more enriched the diners felt, even though in some cases the menus ran to eight courses, butlers and footmen served the food, top hats were worn by the men, and velvet capes were fashionable for the ladies. The following is Ward McAllister's recipe for a successful picnic in the 1870s when he was the veritable arbiter of society:

...to convey any idea of our country parties, one must in detail give the method of getting them up: Riding on the avenue on a lovely summer's day, I would be stopped by a beautiful woman, in gorgeous array, looking so fascinating that if she were to ask you to attempt the impossible, you would at least make the effort. She would open on

me as follows: "My dear friend, we are all dying for a picnic. Can't you get one up for us?"

"Why, my dear lady," I would answer, "you have dinners every day, and charming dinners too; what more do you want?"

"Oh, they're not picnics. Anyone can give dinners," she would reply. "What we want is one of your picnics. Now, my dear friend, do get one up."

This was enough to fire me and set me going. So I reply: "I will do your bidding. Fix on the day at once, and tell me what is the best dish your cook makes."

Out comes my memorandum book, and I write: "Monday, 1 P.M., meet at Narragansett Avenue, bring *filet de boeuf pique*," and with a bow am off in my little wagon, and dash on, to waylay the next cottager, stop every carriage known to contain friends, and ask them, one and all, to join our country party, and assign to each of them the providing of a certain dish and a bottle of champagne. Meeting young men, I charge them to take a bottle of champagne, and a pound of grapes, or order from the confectioner's a quart of ice cream to be sent to me. My pony is put on its mettle; I keep going the entire day getting recruits; I engage my music and servants, and a carpenter to put down a dancing platform, and the florist to adorn it, and that evening I go over in detail the whole affair, map it out as a general would a battle, omitting nothing, not even a salt spoon; I see to it that I have men on the road to direct my party to the farm, and bid the farmer put himself and family, and the whole farm, in holiday attire.

To return to our picnic. The anxiety as to what the weather would be was always my first annoyance, for of course these country parties hinge on the weather. After making all your preparations, everything ready for the start, then to look out of your window in the morning, as I have often done, and see the rain coming down in torrents is far from making you feel cheerful. But, as a rule, I have been most fortunate in my weather. We would meet at Narragansett Avenue at 1 P.M. and all drive out together. On reaching the picnic grounds, I had an army of skirmishers, in the way of servants, thrown out to take from each carriage its contribution to the country dinner. The band would strike up, and off the whole party would fly in the waltz, while I was directing the icing of the champagne and arranging the tables; all done with marvelous celerity.

Then came my hour of triumph, when, without giving the slightest signal (fearing someone might

Eastfair, built between 1929 and 1932, is a privately owned castle, with a moat, a parterre garden, a vineyard; and inside, medieval tapestries, armor, and furnishings.

16

forestall me and take off the prize), I would dash in among the dancers, secure our society queen, and lead with her the way to the banquet. Now began the fun in good earnest. The clever men of the party would assert their claims to the best dishes, proud of the efforts of their cook, loud in their praise of their own game pie, which most probably was brought out by some third party, too modest to assert and push his claim. Beauty was there to look upon, and wit to enliven the feast. The wittiest of men was then in his element, and I only wish I dared quote here his brilliant sallies. The beauty of the land was also there, and all feeling that they were on a frolic, they threw hauteur, ceremonial, and grand company manners aside, and, in place, assumed a spirit of simple enjoyment. Toasts were given and drunk, then a stroll in pairs, for a little interchange of sentiment, and then the whole party made for the dancing platform, danced, till sunset. As at a "Meet," the arrivals and departures were a feature of the day. Four-in-hands, tandems, and the swellest of Newport turn-outs rolled by you. At these entertainments you formed lifetime intimacies with the most cultivated and charming men and women of this country.

McAllister's picnics owed a lot of their jollity to his Yacht Club rum punch—it was made from old plantation rum poured into huge cut-crystal bowls with a large block of ice added to each bowl as the only liquid. "Except when I would pour a bottle of champagne in, which did it no injury."

Newport has simmered down since the heyday of all-out ostentation, and outdoor parties tend to be in a more human scale. The following invitation is a perfect example of how a seasonal delight provides a good excuse for giving a party:

We hope you will join us in enjoying an inhalation of that rarest and most delicate of all natural perfumes, which our beloved Lindens bring to us, for a few precious days each year, at the time of their flowering. That moment is now with us and will remain so until the next high wind sweeps the blossoms away and we will have to wait for the next flowering in 1981. It is because of the threat of wind that we are inviting you with such short notice.

Join us between 5:00 and 8:00 P.M.
on Wednesday, July 23, at Avalon.

It will be a delightful experience, which we wish to share with you. It goes without saying it will be accompanied by appropriate spiritual refreshments to celebrate the occasion.

Kindest regards,

Candy and Jimmy

The seasonal pleasures of summer are so short, just like the blooms of the linden trees, that it is a great joy to be able to extend the time to well beyond Labor Day. An American invention, rather like the English conservatory, is the sun porch, an improvisation that keeps the look of summer all year long. Sometimes called "Florida rooms," they are informal sitting rooms, always bright and cheerful, that actually evolved from front porticoes: In the middle of the eighteenth century there were few professional architects in America, and subsequently the Colonial style for grand houses was copied from England, where it was properly called Georgian. The style encompassed impressive porticoes and thick columns at the entrances. Perhaps because the summer sun was hotter here than in England, the Colonists began to enlarge their front porticoes, making them deeper and more imposing. Soon builders began to design extensions running the length of the houses. The protrusions were no longer porticoes; they had evolved into piazzas, in many cases double-storied ones. The style was an American original, and in architectural terms front protuberances were called piazzas; side protuberances were verandas; small, less imposing extensions were known as porches. Whatever the name, whether in the front, side, or back of the house, they were practical and soon became a way of summer life. That highly respected American tastemaker, A. J. Downing, believed that any country house in the United States was intolerable without some sort of a veranda. He wrote lyrically that they should express "elegance and comfort, picturesqueness and domesticity in design." And the picturesqueness of gingerbread carpentry did indeed make wondrous varieties—the Stick Style is the prototype of the porches that had such a tremendous influence in moving Americans outdoors.

At first the veranda was spartanly furnished with one or two rocking chairs, as its main purpose was for shade and coolness, or for promenades in inclement weather. Downing did suggest in his 1850 book, *The Architecture of Country Houses*, that there were other uses: "dinner being over, the dessert might be served there, and gentlemen addicted to the soothing indulgence of a fragrant 'Havana,' would find the pavillion the best of smoking apartments."

Oak Bluffs cottages are confections for the eye, with gingerbread and Gothic Revival embellishments, gaily painted like cakes that have been freshly iced and decorated.

Pretty picnics have all the amenities of home, along with the joys of a
perfect day, in a perfect spot with some amusing livestock attending the
feast. The woolly ram and the life-size cows are standup constructions
used to decorate fields and lawns—modern expressions of folk art, as
American as quilts and floorcloths. Cows by Woody Jackson; ram and
painted canvas floorcloth by Veva Crozer. All from the Webb & Parsons
Gallery in New Canaan, Connecticut.

Jimmy Goslee's way of entertaining is to throw down big floor pillows, unfold lacquer trays, and add tiny vases of flowers to make a very elegant picnic that is a splash of bold color against nature's green.

24

The Sherrills' veranda epitomizes summer with wicker furniture, hanging baskets, and a charming profusion of plants.

Especially comfortable with a circle of easy chairs, the enclosed porch works well as an extra sitting room and game room. The dazzle of yellow splashed outside on the awning and side curtains heightens the sunny effect. Photograph by Kim Sargent.

Light and airy wicker furniture and an outside awning seem to enlarge and widen a narrow sun porch that runs the length of the house. The wall of sliding glass doors, two seating groups, plus a dining area make it the most useful room for expansive entertaining. Photograph by Kim Sargent.

Open to the ocean, the sun-room at Rock Cliff, which runs the whole
fifty-four-foot length of the living room, is the informal and congenial
gathering place for small groups. The furniture is rattan covered in cotton
canvas; the flooring is biscuit-colored tile laid with straw matting. A
sliding side door goes out to the pool area, which is edged with pink
impatiens.

Porch furniture took on artful airs after the Victorians fell in love with wicker and made the ornate wovenwork a favorite decorating style outside as well as in. Perhaps because the wicker was so curvy and light, it seemed the natural furniture to complement porch latticework and fancy jigsaw work. In summer, families sat on their porches and rocked away the evening in what doctors called "digestive chairs." The healthy as well as homey wicker rocker was another American invention that became a symbol of the good life. The artist Eric Sloane described the family pastime with nostalgia:

> I can't forget the childhood evenings I spent on the long porch of our summer place. As night took over, we would light sticks of fragrant punk to drive away the flying insects. The burning sticks created a series of tiny, gyrating crimson lights as the ladies swayed back and forth in their rocking chairs, and father's cigar was a larger and less active light at the far end of the porch—families actually said things to one another as rockers squeaked an accompaniment.

It was not long before mosquitoes won the battle for the outdoors, and by the early 1900s most of America had given up open-porch sitting at night: the old-fashioned porches were first screened, and then to prolong their usefulness, they were enclosed with glass panels to become sun porches, our informal living rooms dedicated to the look of summer.

SUMMER HOUSES

OLD FARM

**Renovation and development
by Renny Reynolds;
Photographs by Michael Skott**

*The fieldstone house was first built in
1723, added on to in 1793, and except
for modern plumbing, electricity, and a
kitchen has not been changed
architecturally since then.*

Down on the farm each day starts with the sun, but the guinea hens and roosters are up well before that, clucking and crowing for food; then too, Millie and Lilly, Baba and Blanch, Orchid and Violet are clamoring for their breakfast. And so the farmer's chores begin, feeding chickens, dogs, goats, burros, horses, cats, lambs, all the assorted and hungry livestock.

It is not everybody's dream to have a farm and have to spend every summer weekend taking care of animals, clearing the land, zapping poison ivy, pulling weeds out of the vegetable garden, dredging the pond, mucking out the stalls and painting the barns, and so forth. But to the farmer-owner of this property it was a dream come true when he bought thirty acres of overgrown trees and shrubs, six dilapidated outbuildings, and a nice old (run-down) house dating back to 1723. He had searched a year and a half for just the right rural spread to acquire, with enough land available to satisfy his landscaping ambitions and to keep him busy for a long, long time. As far as he is concerned, the longer it takes to design and develop, the better he likes it—the opportunity to till and toil and sculpt the land is each summer's primary focus.

The first summer was devoted to cutting down overgrown trees and saving others from being choked by vines, to restoring barns, activating the pond, making a vegetable and flower garden, along with plotting masses of perennial color splashes for the future. A gazebo was built for the pond, the vegetable garden got a manly scarecrow and a white-painted Victorian fence, and the barn was topped with a bell tower. For all the progress there were, unfortunately, a few setbacks because of the livestock—the ducks ate all the lilies in the pond; Petunia (the pig) crashed out of her pen and trampled a bank of freshly planted flowers; Gertrude and Alice (the goats) decimated the front garden in one quick half-hour spree. But still, for the first summer, the harvest was a bountiful one of berries, vegetables, salad greens, plus profusions of zinnias, dahlias, sunflowers, marguerites, and plenty of herbs.

As for the house, the owner has not spent much time thinking about decorating it. So far he feels it is comfortable without having any pretensions. The favorite room (and the most used) is the sun porch, which runs the length of the house and is adjacent to the kitchen. It is the favorite gathering place, featuring a lovely view that dips and curves over the rolling land. When the owner sits there, he sees not only the beauty of what has been accomplished up to now but also the joy promised by each summer to come.

The farm's entrance plaque is circled with twined grapevine—masses of it have been cleared from the old trees on the property and utilized to make fences.

Petunia, a baby when she came to the farm, is a hefty 350 pounds now; her pen has a pink overhead light bulb and the walls are hung with framed pictures of Miss Piggy.

36

Livestock is everywhere; here two kittens find a comfortable spot for napping. The two "toms" roam the territory at will, often escorting visitors to the front door. In the background is the chicken coop bordered by an herb garden.

A gingerbread fence neatly encloses the vegetable garden; clumps of dahlias are planted at the posts.

A straw scarecrow with patchwork pants and a gingham shirt is attached to a forked tree limb that is stuck in the ground.

The back porch has old-fashioned rattan and wicker furniture covered in cotton, oleander trees in the corners, and at the end of the porch a topiary giraffe is shaped with a fig vine and stands up in a box of gravel.

A picnic by the pond is a peaceful setting, with the newly built gazebo,
designed by the owner in an imitation of an old one, in the background.

THE SMALL HOUSE

**Architect, Henry Melich;
Interior design by Imogene
Taylor of Colefax & Fowler;
Photographs by Kim Sargent**

*The Small House's crisp exterior is
neatly defined with calamondin orange
trees in tubs marching alongside the
geometric walkway, and behind the
tall hedge is a secret garden that can be
seen only from the upstairs balcony.
The large parking area to the left of
the front entrance is minimized with a
hopscotch design of paving stones,
brick, and grass.*

There is something so very satisfactory about taking a tumbled-down forgotten place and turning it into a perfect little gem with just the right ambience. Bringing a place up to scratch, especially a place so far gone and with so little merit, is a labor of love—and once finished it can be the most endearing house to those who have cared enough to suit it to their style of living.

The Small House, gay, sunny, and just right for two, is a lively example of tailoring to a T. After it was bought, the owners had to cart out twenty-seven truckloads of overgrowth before they could see what they had. And not only was the outside a sorry mess, the house itself was in very poor shape, with no front hall, no proper bedrooms (the former owners slept outside on a sleeping porch), no real space for dining, and certainly no place for overnight guests.

The conversion began by moving the end wall of the house out ten feet to accommodate a breakfast room and to enlarge the dining room. That was just the beginning. The creation of something out of nothing really began in earnest when the maze of small, inadequate rooms was transformed into more comfortable spaces.

The Small House is still a doll's house, but there is a proper front hall now, a separate guest cottage, and a glorious gazebo room of airy latticework used for lunches and candlelight dinners. The plan is simple: the living room has two front windows (one of which was originally the front door) and joins onto the cardroom, an enclosed loggia that opens out to the terrace and garden. The dining room is adjacent, as is the breakfast room with its sliding glass doors that connect to the gazebo party room.

The outdoors is in and the inside has the feeling of being a part of the garden, a very happy arrangement that gives the house its sunny spirit. With tall hedges creating a walled courtyard, the compound has become a miniature villa, with trellised additions and little pocket gardens tucked around a terrace, an expansive green lawn, and a swimming pool. Throughout the garden the planting is in depth, with areas of flowers massed together in one strong color for maximum impact. The ingenious architectural plan makes every bit of the space count so that one believes it is much larger, a trick of design that also manages to balance color and form beautifully.

Embracing the outside as it does, and with sunlight and fresh flowers enhancing the inside, the rooms are always bright and smiling. Crisp chintzes are in delicious colors; sofa and chair contours are rounded and plumply soft for lush comfort; and details found in frills and furbelows are a visual delight. The house has a young, candy box newness with just enough old-fashioned charms and Victorian airs to give it a homey, settled-in look.

In the hedge-bordered front garden curving grass paths swirl around islands of fruit trees; the ornamental terra-cotta planters have been colorfully bordered with gerbera daisies. The patterning of the bricks was inspired by a Roman mosaic floor.

Tucked in a corner of the hall is a welcoming cat and a garden-in-a-basket. Growing out of the moss are ivies, ferns, caladiums, and orchids.

In the living room blue strié-painted walls give a pale, cool background for lively chintzes patterned with sharp green and kumquat yellow. Dressmaker touches in ruching and ruffles, masses of flowers, and lacy ferns add to the softness. The plump banquette sofa curves along one wall, helping the small room to expand its seating capacity.

A corner of the dining room is a vignette of color playing among the patterns, pictures, and porcelains. A collection of bird and botanical prints is grouped on fabric-covered walls; the honey-suckle pattern is a delightful background for the delicately painted Adam chairs and the tier table filled with Davenport china.

A sleeping porch was transformed into an upstairs sitting room with white wicker furniture, gaily sprigged chintz, and a lively documentary wallpaper.

In the guesthouse a bedroom of rose pinks and misty blues is dramatically vaulted with painted beams. It has a hospitable, old-fashioned air, with antique iron beds freshened up with shiny blue paint.

To connect the guesthouse with the main house, an area was trellised and topped with a criss-crossing of lofty beams. Stephanotis is being trained overhead.

50

The gazebo party room is a Victorian dream of shadow and light, a soaring ceiling with graceful arches, hanging baskets of flowers, and exotic trees. When the sun filters through the tentlike trellised ceiling onto the brick floor, it makes a magical design.

Lots of clipped greenery, manicured and clustered into patterns, harmonize the garden with the pool and the gazebo party room. The design provides eye-catching areas to make the expanse seem larger, and at the same time it gives serenity and privacy.

A little latticed pavillion at the end of the garden is a focal point housing orchid plants. The incredible sculpture inside is fashioned in fantastic eighteenth-century grotto style—a terra-cotta mermaid splashing on frothy waves made of coral and seashells.

ROCK
CLIFF

**Interior design by
William Hodgins**

*Rock Cliff overlooks the ocean with a
lawn that sweeps to the very edge of
Newport's cliffs.*

When Rock Cliff was photographed in the 1870s for architect George Chaplin Mason's book *Newport and Its Cottages*, the house was half-timbered, with overhanging stories, roofs of various heights, balconies and bays, piazzas, and a porte cochere. By 1910 all that homey exterior carpentry work was gone, replaced by stucco and stone, pillars and pediments, and some very grand eighteenth-century-style detailing. It became a stately mansion when it was renovated by Mason's son in the style of Louis XVI; classical moldings and cornices now decorate the large rooms with their long, tall windows opening to spectacular views. Looking from the inside out, the house seems to float on top of the ocean, for its green lawn goes right to the cliffs that line the coast. In a high wind, when the surf beats on the rocks below, the ocean spray comes up almost to the stone balustrades of the terrace.

But even on rough days when the wind howls, all is serene at Rock Cliff. The inside mechanism is orderly and soothing; it is a house run on well-oiled wheels with a generous capacity for entertaining. The excellent staff keeps the place at peak performance. Georgie, who has been with the family for forty-five years, is the mainstay. He wears a spanking white coat, serves at table, and makes perfect martinis and superb daiquiris. Anne is the general over all; she keeps the larder filled, tends the gardens, both vegetable and cutting, and arranges magnificent bouquets of flowers. Michael, who trained in Paris, is the chef. Others clean and help out at parties. Every morning the yardman rakes the driveway gravel into smooth swirls. With all this routine maintenance and detailed attention, it would seem that life at Rock Cliff might be rather stuffy and rigid; on the contrary, the atmosphere is gay and lively, in the spirit of happy summers filled with visiting children and grandchildren, picnics on the rocks, sailing, and windsurfing.

It is a house for having fun. It is also a house for attractive people; the colors are soft and complementary to blue eyes, fair skin, blond hair. In the decorations little details are notable: curtains are lined, sometimes double-lined, with a complementary fabric and then edged with a ruching or braid. Bed skirts have been made in the same meticulous way. Much of the furniture is hand-painted to resemble wood or marble; some pieces were especially overscaled to diminish the size of the rooms. Even though there are beautiful French, English, and American antiques everywhere, the look is not "period" or stiffly formal. The overall effect is completely light and buoyant, a place warmed with golden light, the reflection of sun and sea.

The front hall, splendidly detailed with fine moldings and generous proportions, opens airily with French doors to the library, living, and dining rooms. The hand-painted wallpaper panel of a mountain scene is by Zuber. The stylish geometric flooring is of black walnut and fir woods.

A handsome, rich emerald green envelops the library, a night room used by the family mostly as a cozy sitting room. The Regency-style chairs were hand-painted by Yorke Kennedy. The replica of the owner's yacht, Tantra, seen silhouetted against the far wall, was made by Tom Gouzoules. Inside the model the interior is completely furnished with banquettes, tables, pictures, and flowers.

In the huge living room the palette of soft colors casts a light that seems to wash the room with a perpetual sunny glow. The dimensions are so spacious that the area holds three sofas, two settees, ten chairs, six benches, and four potted trees without looking a bit crowded. The room is divided in half by a big round table covered with a yellow linen cloth and piled with books. On the far wall near the marble fireplace is a painting on gold leaf called Rising Sun by William Chewning. Beyond, glass doors open into the sun-room.

Reflected in the mirror in the living room is a carved, gilded eagle that perches on top of a French clock of the 1870s.

The dining room, which looks out to sea, is the frosting on the cake, with its graceful nineteenth-century American crystal chandelier that came from the governor's mansion in Pennsylvania. The silk taffeta curtains were deliberately left unlined, to float and billow with the breezes. The Duncan Phyfe dining table seats ten, and with extra leaves, sixteen. And for big dinners, the addition of round tables and gold party chairs enables the room to accommodate fifty.

Peaches and cream flow together to tint a charming bedroom in the most delicate hues. The four-poster bed with carved pineapple finials has been expertly painted by Yorke Kennedy with blue draperies on the headboard. A television set hides in the blue cabinet on the far wall painted by Robert Jackson with floral insets and faux-bamboo detailing.

Details of the bed showing the decorative painting by Yorke Kennedy. Photographs by Edward Oleksak.

MILL
POND
HOUSE

**Interior design by
the Francis Kelloggs**

*An inherited boyhood home, now
turned into a summer retreat and
cattle farm, was first painted pink in
the 1920s.*

A gentle rolling landscape like a pocket version of a vast country estate in England is the setting for Mill Pond House. There are acres and acres of glorious land filled with pastures and ponds, hundreds of old trees, and dry stone walls meandering throughout. The place goes back a long way—the first recorded deed was a conveyance in 1713 of the gristmill on Stone Hill River together with the surrounding acreage.

The owner grew up at Mill Pond House in the 1920s, and when his parents died, he inherited the estate. He came home to it after World War II expecting all of his boyhood memories to come to life, like opening a familiar scrapbook. The reality was different: instead of the wonderful vistas and rolling fields he remembered, there was now just a jungle of overgrowth. In what he thought was a brilliant solution, he put sheep out to graze to devour the vines and brambles quickly and thus bring some order back to the land. The sheep did eat away at the problem, but in the process caused bigger problems with the neighbors by straying into adjoining gardens and raising havoc. Finally, a herd of Dexter cattle, the smallest in the world (and unable to get over the low stone fences), was imported from England to finish the job. Now the Dexters are part of the landscape at Mill Pond House, looking like big sleek dogs roaming the pastures.

Mill Pond House, which overlooks the pastures, gives no indication in front that it has any view at all, being originally a three-room farmhouse on a main road. Once you are inside, however, the house opens up beautifully to the surrounding hollows and hillocks.

There have been many additions and changes since the 1920s: rooms were expanded, porches added and then enclosed, fireplaces changed around, gardens relocated. But the look and the mood of the place have remained the same. The nucleus of early American pieces was the start, then the family's treasures collected through the years added another dimension to the good, simple furniture. The pictures in the house are mostly photographs and paintings by the owner's mother, and there is lots of needlework around to warm the rooms, even a hooked rug commemorating the first Dexter bull to arrive at the farm. It is family-style decorating at its best, done with a sense of history and a blend of simplicity and sophistication.

Pictured are the owner and his wife, who labor hard to maintain the sprawling 100-acre property.

A black swan glides on the pond over the shadowy reflection of the pink house.

The sawmill house, called Miller's Mill, was rebuilt in 1920; the original structure was a gristmill dating from 1713. Early in the nineteenth century the original stone grain grinders were replaced by a wrought-iron saw about seven feet in length. The sawmill still exists, together with the water chutes and cast-iron paddle wheels that provided the power to cut timber for over half a century.

The view from the living room is a verdant panorama of valleys and hills and lofty trees, seen over a platform deck planted with pinks, reds, and shades of green, and guarded by a rabbit and a squirrel.

The terrace, suspended over the lawn, the beautiful old boxwood, and the pond, is ideal for afternoon tea.

An oil painting of Mill Pond House was done in 1937 by the owner's mother, Emily Baker Kellogg.

The children always called this room "the chicken room" because a stuffed chicken sits on a nest of eggs by the fireplace, and little oil paintings of roosters and hens are tucked around. There is even a clock in the shape of a chicken. Beyond the bookcase glass doors open onto the long living room. The banquette, covered in baize green, is a telephone corner with windows onto the dining porch. This room is one of the three original ones in the farmhouse, which dates back to the late 1700s.

There are ninety-four bird pictures in the living room, an extraordinary collection of ornithologically correct bird collages pieced together with fancy needlework and bits of material. They were sewn in the eighteenth century over a period of forty years by Hannah Pettigrew for her sister, and the collection was discovered in an antiques shop bound into a leather book.

The forty-foot-long paneled living room was added in 1910, with wide oak flooring, lots of windows, and glass doors opening onto the terrace and the garden side. The fireplace, which used to be at the end of the room, was moved to the center between the pair of camelback sofas. Having ample space, easy and relaxing, the room is openhearted and inviting with its rich endowment of early American pine, cherry, and maple furniture. Many of the antiques were collected by the owner's mother in the early 1900s. The printed Belgian linen was added over thirty years ago against the advice of a decorator friend, who warned never to put a splashy fabric on sofa and chairs and certainly never at windows.

One of the original rooms of the house is a little gallery space used for small dinners. The whole back wall is ingeniously covered with an oil painting by Emily Baker Kellogg of the owner's great-grandfather's house on the Hudson River. Curiously, one side of the house is in Mississippi steamboat style; the other Greek Revival. In the winter the lake in front provided the owner with a side business known as the Knickerbocker Ice Company, which delivered large blocks of ice to clubs and restaurants in New York.

This was the children's sleeping porch, known as the "TB sanitorium," and it was glassed in after World War II to make a dining room. The blue-painted grandfather clock was one of many collected and restored by the owner's father, whose hobby was clocks. The pair of Windsor armchairs, and there are also eight Windsor side chairs in the collection, came from a house in Maine whose entire contents were bought by the owner's mother in the 1920s.

The upstairs master bedroom overlooks the garden on one side and the pond on the other. The red-and-white patterns in florals and geometrics make a cheerful background for the traditional early American furniture. The 200-year-old rug is reversible; the watercolor of spruce trees was painted by the owner's mother.

The swimming pool was added in 1952; the octagonal pool pavillion, designed by the owner, was built in 1955 and seems to float on the property. Inside it is equipped with a kitchen, bathhouses, and 1930s rattan furniture. The black forms on the other side of the fence are Dexter cattle roaming by.

78

A bower of green, with trees as walls and lush grass as carpeting, is for
alfresco lunching by the pool.

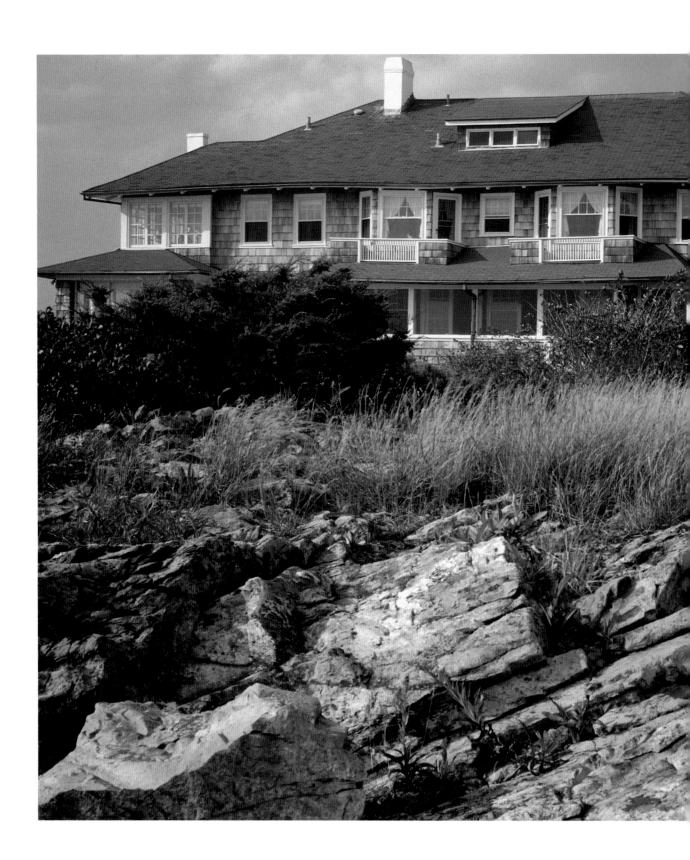

BAY
HOUSE

**Interior design by
Mark Hampton**

*Bay House sprawls generously by the
sea and is very much a part of the
powerful rocky terrain.*

Bay House, completed in 1917, was hailed by Antoinette F. Downing and Vincent J. Scully, Jr., in *The Architectural Heritage of Newport, Rhode Island* (1967) as "one of the sole echoes of a continuing tradition of free architectural design in Newport."

Free from whatever influences, then, Bay House now is also free-spirited inside. "Everything is brand-new here, all store-bought," says the owner—well, not everything, but enough of the furnishings and pictures do constitute a new beginning for an old house. The owner wanted an unfrivolous, workable house, without prissiness or fussy things, no eighteenth-century French furniture, or anything at all not in keeping with a summer-by-the-sea residence. Because he had grown up here, he knew exactly what he did not want—a very formal atmosphere. The resulting style is uncomplicated; there is nothing fragile or too precious to worry about, yet the house has the dignity of neat design and orderliness. It accommodates a bevy of summer activities: there are always lots of children running in and out with wet feet and dripping buckets; fishing, waterskiing, and wind-surfing are their favorite sports; and a picnic or a giant clambake on the rocks is the family's preferred entertainment. And with all this, there are also houseguests and busloads of cousins who come and go. Because the place gets a lot of wear and tear, everything has to be substantial and easily cared for.

The focus is on good-looking, solid furniture, with some antiques, and some pieces especially made; and with a monochromatic color scheme. The colors are driftwood and pebble tones, some sharpened with a jolt of warm blue; the walls are honeyed or pale cream; the pictures are watery pastels or graceful abstractions in subtle shades; the floors are covered with straw or woven cotton rugs. It is tranquil, except for the dining room, whose walls are a lively red dominated by a gloriously rococo Flemish still life. Upstairs, too, there is surprise: one of the bedrooms has a 1930s mirrored bed, a glamorous movie-star-like model of beveled glass fashioned into sweetheart curves. It is the Bridal Suite, and next to it is the Quaker Room, a spare bedroom done very quietly in pine.

The owner says that Bay House has its own ghosts and special noises: "It sighs when we come for the summer and seems to swell with warmth, and then when we leave, it seems to expire, in another deep sigh, probably with relief that we've gone."

A beautiful feature of the front hall is its broad and commodious opening onto spacious rooms facing east, south, and west.

84

The double living room is washed with mellow sand and stone colors and comfortably furnished with three seating groups. The bold floral chintz mixes well with the geometrics, stripes, and textures of the room. All the fabrics are cotton for easy care; the rugs are hand-woven cottons, too.

The cheery dining room is a happy mélange of American pieces, reproduction chairs, a French marble mantel, and a glorious seventeenth-century Flemish still life.

Being in the master bedroom is like being at sea, looking out from the upper deck of a houseboat. The mood is quiet and uncluttered, the room distinguished with some good American pine, maple, and walnut pieces. The oversize chaise, made in two parts, was designed by the owner.

Purely feminine and just right for a young girl, this bed-sitting room is prettied up with polka-dotted walls and a romantic chintz blooming with cabbage roses. The flowered frieze near the ceiling ties the room together like party gift wrapping.

POOL HOUSE

Interior design by Letitia Gates

An old horse-and-buggy barn was transformed into a little jewel for summer living. Long windows cost three dollars each at a junk shop, and a carpenter turned them into bays with new framing. The French doors were also a thrifty find; the owner gave the wood a pinkish tone, and her dog did the antiquing by scratching to get in.

A "shoestring operation" is what the owner calls her decorating. "Something from nothing" could also be an apt description of the rags-to-riches look that comes off so beautifully in the Pool House.

And it is just that—an island house (with no view) that boasts a lot of space for entertaining plus a large swimming pool and terrace. The pool also has an adjacent cabana done up in wicker and sailcloth and outfitted with a compact kitchen.

It is very unpretentious and casual; rather like a little house to the manner born, structured on good bones and fleshed out with a spirited mix of new acquisitions and old attic stuff, together with some talented sleights of hand.

The house began as a horse-and-buggy barn. The downstairs space was turned into two big sitting rooms, one with a dining area and kitchen; the other with a breakfast room that also doubles as a guest bedroom and bath; and the upstairs hay loft became the bedroom. It is all very contained, very leisurely, and it opens pleasantly to the outdoors.

There is brick flooring throughout, ingeniously laid by the owner with the help of a how-to manual and a handyman. Windows, mantels, and doors were bought from wrecking companies or thrift shops. A lot of the furniture and china came from hotels' going-out-of-business sales and the mundane chairs, bureaus, and wardrobes were spruced up with decorative painting. Even the chintz, inherited with some of the sofas and chairs, got a painting over: some of the flowers were recolored with acrylic paints. The result is bright and genial, with some clever trompe-l'oeil effects transforming ordinary pieces into special delights.

The hayloft-into-bedroom doubles its space with mirroring and features the bath—a tub is settled into the corner niche, making the spa a prettied-up part of the room. Curtaining, along with the bedcovers, was made of sheeting fabric. The old French sleigh bed was first antiqued white and fabric was then tacked to it with a staple gun. A toy chest at the foot of the bed is used as the linen closet.

93

The bedroom commode was gessoed and then decorated with geraniums
in acrylic paints.

Looking over the loft bedroom railing is like peering into a corner of a
baronial mansion. The delicate crystal chandelier and the buffalo horns
are eccentric touches that delight. The Gothic-shaped windows, a
wrecking-company buy, add to the spirit of the room.

94

An armoire used for linens and party china is dressed up with the owner's trompe-l'oeil painting.

A screen copied from the famous tapestries in the Cluny Museum in Paris is part of
the Old World charm of the dining-sitting room where blue and white in porcelain, chintz,
and a Chinese rug meld together. On either side of the front door there is more trompe-l'oeil
decorative painting by the owner.

The expansive room beyond the dining area opens onto a terrace and
pool. All is airy and light, with cotton slipcovers hiding a pair of leggy
Louis XV armchairs and chintz made brighter by the owner's repainting
the flowers a soft color.

A small room adjacent to the two small living rooms makes an intimate dining space, and with a Murphy bed tucked in the corner it also doubles as a guestroom. The ceiling is covered with a sprigged sheeting fabric that is delightfully summery, and it is also used for the curtains. The owner has decorated the trumeau mirror with a motif taken from the fabric.

The pool house pavillion is gaily painted with trompe-l'oeil orange trees
that grow out of jardinieres up onto the tray ceiling. The shells on either
side of the windows are lights.

A kitchen unit housing a stove, a sink, and china cabinets is made to look like a display cabinet with artful antiquing and decorative painting.

SUMMER-HOUSE

Architect, Peter Paul Muller;
Contractor, Jacqueline Scott;
Interior design by
Blanche Greenstein
and Thos. K. Woodard

Summerhouse, originally built in 1939, is brightened with new paint and masses of geraniums and zinnias.

The house had been empty a long time; it was run-down and forlorn, with waist-high weeds, a broken window, shingles missing—and nobody ever came near the place. After looking at it for a while, the couple next door, who were staying in a summer rental, persuaded themselves that they should save the place from total ruin. Even though they had recently bought property to build on, the little tumbledown shack appealed to them. They liked the country feeling of the area—the beach was only a block away—and the house had a nice sloping roofline. It really seemed that giving the old house new life would be an easier project than building a house from scratch.

The couple, who were involved in running a shop and writing a book at the same time, did buy the house. They found out that it had been built in 1939 by the farmer who had lived in it and raised his family there. It turned out that the timing was perfect for both parties, as he had moved away and abandoned the place long ago. Because the house was situated on a small plot of land and had a dark, mildewed interior, it was purchased at a bargain.

The rebirth of the house began in earnest when the new owners sat inside one beautiful day and realized that with more windows and fewer walls they could have exactly what they wanted in a summer home: lots of space and lots of light. They were against creating a replica of an old saltbox because they knew the design would be too inward-oriented, making the interiors too dim for their liking, and they were definitely not in favor of the opposite extreme: large expanses of plate-glass walls. The idea was to let the sunshine in and still keep the country charm of the house; they did just that by adding new windows between the old ones, plus putting in a big skylight. When most of the walls were knocked down, the house was extended four feet out at the back, allowing a kitchen, and an expansion of the upstairs attic into two bedrooms and a bath. The renovation took from November through May and, surprisingly, it was kept within their modest budget. It was so unusual that the owners were once thinking of naming their house A Miracle.

The structure has some interesting angles to it—there are unexpected niches and storage hideaways—and some clever recycling: the old doors of the house were cut up and made into board-and-batten ones; leftover wood was fashioned into doorknobs and curtain rods. There are also some special touches that lend quality: the kitchen cabinets were hand-made of cedar, and the flooring throughout was constructed of wide pine boards put together with square nails. All the woods used in the house have a whitewashed, scrubbed finish to soften the color, and the bleached effect not only gives a pristineness to the rooms but also adds enormously to the airy setting. The result is pure simplicity through the use of honest materials.

Being enthusiastic collectors, the owners are always adding and changing the patterns, colors, and textures in the house. The clean and unobtrusive background is very receptive to this kind of decorating, and consequently there is a strong focus on the objects and the elements themselves. The rooms are treated as compositions of Americana, which is a splendid way of showing off favored new acquisitions. Their spontaneity lies in the assortment of things that are souvenirs of American life, delightful as well as decorative. It is a display of history along with a deep enjoyment of design.

Crazy City is the title of the marvelous pieced quilt dated 1885 that hangs over the mantel in the living room, the largest room in the house, which flows into a dining area and kitchen. Note how some of the colors and shapes in the quilt are reflected and enlarged in the handsome antique rag rug.

C. WINNE.

CRAZY.
CITY. 1885.

105

The honey and flax tones are all the basic background colors needed for the owners' changing collections of Americana. For variety, the owners often have nothing on their fireplace wall (except the play of sunshine), and they display crockery or baskets on the mantelpiece. In this version of this spacious room a framed Amish crib quilt is the important design element, and blue-and-white spongeware pitchers decorate the mantel.

In the living room, looking from the front door down through to the dining area, the space is rather like an art gallery, showing off the collected patterns and textures that make up the decorating philosophy in the house. There are Indian baskets, painted boxes, tinware, and a crib quilt framed as a picture. The Windsor chairs are all old; the chandelier is a reproduction of tin and wood. Here, and throughout the house, the curtains of linen and cotton hang in the simplest way from tabs looped over dowels.

A little attic bedroom is exuberant with pure country furnishings and a mix of gay patterns. The small-scale sofa dates from around 1830; the bed quilt, from around 1860. The New England cupboard and rocker both retain their original paint.

A skylight brightens an even smaller guestroom that is fastidiously simple and alive with the spirit of the American past. The chairs stand as strong design elements, almost like sculptures. The bed quilt is in the Flower Basket design and was made about 1880. A particularly commodious basket, woven with wooden struts and filled with books and magazines, serves as the bedside catchall.

Alive with color and pattern, the stenciled guestroom is particularly beautiful and is always treated to different quilts for the beds, but never matching ones as the diversity of their colors and patterns makes the room more interesting. The handsome and imaginative stenciling was created by artist Virginia Teichner, who also made the stenciled tiebacks for the plain curtains.

109

THE
WHIM

**Interior design by
Tom Hagerman**

*This gardener's cottage, modestly boxlike
on the outside, opens up to unexpected
sophistication and luxury.*

Personality makes this summer house a delight and a surprise. It began as a modest gardener's cottage that was part of a large seaside estate; then it swelled out, with the new expansion encompassing the eight-car garage next door.

From garage-into-grandeur took about ten years of planning in order to make the design accommodate a large living room, a library, and an office downstairs, with four large bedrooms above. To allocate the spaces, the garage was paced off and rooms were chalked in place, as were the windows and doors; but that was the easy part. Turning the bare boards of the utilitarian car harbor into a gracious house required the longest and the most patient renovation. Fine eighteenth-century moldings and mantels, paneling, and carved friezes provided the backbone of the building's metamorphosis. Finding the "good bones" of the architectural detailing was serendipitous—before they turned over Marble House to the Preservation Society of Newport County for a house museum, the Frederick Princes summered there in an apartment on the top floor. When the mansion was sold, the beautiful woodwork and mantels from the family quarters were put up for auction, and subsequently the pieces found their way to The Whim's garage rooms. To create the atmosphere of an English country home, it took consummate care and attention to detail to juggle and fit the panels and pieces of carved wood into scale and harmony within the space. The gaps and chasms were filled in with expert carpentry work; using pine, mellowed and fashioned to match the original old wood.

The house has style, with its beautiful new packaging, and fortunately the furnishings live up to the splendid background. The interior design is dressy, but very livable, and even with the formality there is no place one can't relax with feet up and a book. Perhaps the hallmark of the house is that everything in it is a memento: the furniture, the pictures—all are family hand-me-downs, the results of attic raids, auction finds, and bargains bought on trips. Having absolutely nothing store-bought is incredible, but what is even more special is the putting together of all the diverse elements into an appealing whole.

The place has a feeling of continuity, of successive periods merging together to give just the right feeling of mellowness. It has assurance, but above all, hospitality and well-being along with a well-groomed appearance. Although little has been changed and nothing refurbished in the fourteen summers since the owner's makeover, the house is still fresh. It is kept immaculately, with brasses gleaming, silver shining, and fragrant bowls of flowers throughout.

The gardener's cottage plus the garage-house addition contains, according to the owner, a hodgepodge of hand-me-downs and auction bargains. The potting shed in back is a decorative little house, trellised with vines and trimmed with hydrangea blue.

113

A playful seal and a graceful eagle preside over the old-fashioned garden, always resplendent with magnificent blooms from June through September. For cutting, there is a rose garden and a separate plot of dahlias and zinnias. The orderly and neatly patterned garden is in sharp contrast to the view beyond, where the lawn breaks into a mass of rocks and the ocean.

114

The living room is symmetrical, with pairs of windows on the far walls, and sliding glass doors on either side of the fireplace opening out to the garden and the sea view beyond. A mix of French and English furniture is comfortably arranged to take full advantage of the magnificent mantelpiece. As the owner says, it is a hodgepodge of acquisitions, some sentimental choices, some imposing antiques, but the way they are put together has great charm and character.

Honey-toned pine paneling and French doors from Newport's Marble House form the opposite side of the room to balance the imposing mantelpiece. The walls are painted pistachio green, a becoming background for the engaging collection of prints, paintings, and family photographs.

Lacquered a claret-wine color, the library is also toned by the mellow glow of the eighteenth-century moldings that give the room its architectural personality. The Venetian secretary adds green and gold tones to the palette of reds and yellows. Family memorabilia and the distinction of the furniture express the mood of the whole house, a blending of originality with tradition.

The dining room is in the gardener's cottage, connected to the garage part of the house by a wide graceful hall. The room is eclectic, with Dutch landscape paintings, hunting scenes, and watercolors of the South. In one corner a French wire birdcage holds stuffed canaries brought back from Thailand, and in the opposite corner sits an eighteenth-century English child's highchair. The unifying elements here are crisp blue-and-white patterns in the fabric and export porcelains.

118

A guest bedroom revels in eccentricity, with walls glazed an unexpected shiny black, the background for a set of exotic nineteenth-century furniture. The Venetian pieces are pine, carved in the grotto style, and before stripping the wood shimmered with silver leaf. The pictures in the room are a collection of delicately painted Indian and Persian subjects.

ISLAND HOUSE

**Interior design by
Mrs. Henry Parish II**

*Four generations of the same family
have summered in this rambling, genial
island house; it is over 150 years old.*

The owner of Island House, Mrs. Henry Parish II, is one of our most influential decorating talents, known for her "undecorated" look and legendary for mixing the grand with the humble, the nostalgic with the new, the homemade craft with the great museum piece. She has the knack of combining luxury and charm. Her eagle eye and unerring instinct lend her rooms a sense of gaiety, a lot of comfort, and enough color, pattern, and texture to add just the right spice. There is fun and whimsy pervading every corner of her house, even the back stairs and the laundry room.

Her home is a top-notch example of how an old and much-loved summer place is made to look fresh and lively for eight grandchildren and lots of other relatives and guests. Comfort is the key, with plenty of plump sofas and chairs, and fluffy afghans always at hand for curling up and reading or napping. Flowers are always in abundance to assail the senses; and clear, crisp colors lift the spirits. Nothing remains static; things are switched around a lot. The tabletops get new objects; flower and plant arrangements are inventive and lavish without being stagey; worn-out fabrics are replaced—never with the same print, but with something different that always blends and marries with what is already there. The house is like a kaleidoscope that continually changes ever so slightly, with just enough difference to keep it on its toes. It is an art. And for a house over 150 years old, this art projects a refreshing young atmosphere while preserving the essential character and harmony of the place.

A circular brick terrace with a low stone wall breaks the broad lawn that sweeps to the bay beyond. Tuberous begonias and impatiens summer here under the grove of trees. Another circular garden, bordered by a hedge of hemlocks, perches at the water's edge.

A *decklike porch edges the house and makes another place for a garden of
container plants: hanging ferns, topiary ivy vines, clematis vines, lilies in
clay pots, white geraniums in tubs, primulus plants tucked into baskets.*

A Victorian birdcage with castlelike
turrets and crenellated edges is an
elegant and decorative structure for the
back porch, which is the breakfast
room, the laundry room, and also the
favorite entrance to the house.

Narrow back stairs are treated to a
painted runner that ends with a
portrait of a marmalade cat dozing on
a needlepoint cushion.

124

Favorite dogs, both carved and painted, share a kitchen corner with spongeware pottery and an old wicker chair embellished with Victorian needlework and an embroidered tea towel.

Just inside the front door is a niche filled with miniature baskets and bottles, little pictures, and porcelain doodads. The carved parrot on his perch, a Gothic side chair with a Guatemalan cushion, the peacock wicker chair from Hong Kong—all seem to live happily together, which proves that what endures in decorating is personal style and taste.

What was once the dining room is now a sitting room that flows into the new addition. All the convivial elements for comfort and ease are here in the decorating—soft chintz, sunny colors, old things, new things, and some surprises: the curtain valances are painted chintz with ribbon rosettes; the flowered cloth over what used to be the dining room table is bordered with carved wooden tassels.

The front parlor is in soft focus, combining old-fashioned floral chintzes, faded rag rugs, and needlepoint pillows together with vintage, carved furniture. The settled, almost timeless look is interrupted by a Victorian rocker lacquered white and upholstered with a handwoven fabric.

The new addition, which has become the dining room, opens up with sliding glass doors and features a painted table that is marbleized and edged with a trompe-l'oeil ribbon design. The straight-back chairs were once golden oak and were part of the original furnishings of the house. The wool carpeting that covers the entire expanse of the sitting room-into-dining room is woven with rainbow stripes.

A tiny guest bedroom, dominated by a luxurious Regency bed, is enveloped in beautiful prints. The combination of stripes and florals gives the little room its punch.

Pinks and reds make a soft glowing background for a very feminine bedroom. The four-poster bed is canopied in delicate lace and covered with an American patchwork quilt.

Rugs on top of rugs, in this case hooked ones laid over straw matting, make a lively pattern to add to the play of different fabrics in the library. The lampshades are Mrs. Parish's decoupage work; the valances are hand-carved of wood.

*In a bedroom an invitingly oversize chaise floats on a rug of blankets that
have been stitched together. Their boldly colored patterns make the room
strikingly contemporary.*

130

Opposite the big chaise in the same room more lavish comfort is to be found in a generously overstuffed sofa and armchair and lots of pillows. The bed hangings and coverlet, slipcovers and curtains are all a medley of prints that blend together expertly.

132

The gardens at Island House are an extravagance
of blooms—the flowers have the most lavish
colors and are in such abundance—making
a glorious summer-long display.

CECILY'S PLACE

Interior design by
Alexandra Stoddard

*Facing the ocean, the house's southern
side takes full advantage of the
splendid view, and with its deck shaped
like a prow, it looks like a large boat
moored on a grassy plot.*

From a narrow, winding dirt road, walled in with tall marsh grass, we come to an isolated spot where bayberries grow on the dunes and beach plums shine in the sun. It is the best of both worlds, a house overlooking a pond *and* the ocean, with salt winds, gray mist, fresh blue water, swans, and swallows all being part of the scenery.

Built of siding, the north face, and entrance, of the house is private, hiding the wondrous views. Once inside, every room opens its arms wide to nature, an ever-changing spectacle where sunsets and moonrises are integral features of the decorating. Situated on a jutting point of land, the layout of the major rooms in the house is almost arrow-straight, all facing south, with a viewing balcony above the combined living room and dining room, the perfect setting for observing the sand and the sky and the sea.

As all the rooms open up to the view, being inside is like living in a vibrant seascape. The walls are sand-colored; the floors and structural crossbeams are cedar; the fabrics are natural fibers of raw silk, cotton, wool, and mohair, mingling nicely with natural wicker furniture.

The colors are cooled down, quiet and earthy, allowing the rooms to breathe in the warmth and excitement of the outdoors. It is a sweep-clean kind of house, easy to care for, and meticulously outfitted with substance, quality, and elements of luxury. The owner, having spent one summer in the house, has decided to extend her stay through the winter months. Curtains have been ordered.

The view from the balcony inside shows the fusion of sand and earth colors. In the daytime, when the sun is strongest, the walls take on a peachy glow; at dusk, the tone changes to a warm stone color. The painting is by Mühl; the white-lacquered candelabra were once iron black.

An easy arrangement of furniture grouped around the raised hearth is oriented to get the best view, or on inclement days, to enjoy a blazing fire. The dining table of lacquered goatskin expands to seat twelve; the chairs are Louis XV copies, hand-carved in oak. The painting on the fireplace wall is by Cathelin.

136

An ice-blue bedroom is frilled with white pillows and a quilt patterned with the colors of crushed fruits; a lacy straw rug and a curlicue wicker chair add to the froth and lightness. The still-life painting over the bed is a Mühl.

A sheltered deck of weathered gray redwood is the outdoor living space, a great bird-watching spot furnished with suntanning mats and backrests. The bird sculpture on the ledge flies with the wind.

Trained at the New York School of Interior Design, PATRICIA CORBIN is a senior editor at *House Beautiful,* who has written two books on design, *All About Wicker* (1978) and *Designers Design for Themselves* (1980).

TED HARDIN is a New York photographer specializing in editorial work for leading fashion and home furnishings magazines.